What people are saying about …

MOVE TOWARD THE MESS

"I highly recommend this book for those who are willing to live out a wildly different and somewhat dangerous kind of Christianity."

Rick Bundschuh, author of *Soul Surfer* and
pastor of Kauai Christian Fellowship

"John Hambrick challenges Christians to move toward the messiest people and situations in life."

Carey Nieuwhof, author of *Lasting Impact*
and pastor of Connexus Church

"*Move Toward the Mess* moves the reader out of apathy and staleness to the messiness of life where we find ourselves engaged and energized in our faith."

Betsy Duffey, author of *The Shepherd's Song*

"John Hambrick cuts through the complacency and clutter that cripple our attempts at changing the world, offering clear and accessible ways to make our faith actionable and our lives remarkable."

Dr. Bill Donahue, professor of
pastoral theology at TIU and author
of *The Irresistible Community*

"John Hambrick helps us hear Jesus's invitation to follow him in new ways and to jump into the messy, life-giving adventure of becoming a part of Jesus's work in our world."

David Rohrer, pastor of Emmanuel Presbyterian Church
and author of *The Sacred Wilderness of Pastoral Ministry*

"What makes *Move Toward the Mess* so compelling is that it reflects Jesus's life, which was an *approach to life* that *brought life.*"

Bill Willits, executive director of Ministry
Environments at North Point Ministries

"This book will prepare your heart, soul, and mind to move into the dangerously fulfilling territory of life to the full … the life Jesus lived and the life he offers us right now."

Seth Condrey, music director at Woodstock City Church

"John Hambrick challenges us to love God and to love people by buckling our seat belts and following Jesus toward the mess."

Tom Haugen, chaplain at Gordon College

"A fresh perspective on shedding religion and finding the Jesus way."

Erin Johnson, success coach

"This book will be a mentor to you, filled with stories and questions that will lead you."

Scott Cormode, Hugh De Pree professor of
leadership development at Fuller Seminary

MOVE TOWARD THE MESS

THE ULTIMATE FIX FOR A BORING CHRISTIAN LIFE

JOHN HAMBRICK

David C Cook®
transforming lives together

To Patty, John, and Carrell
Words fail. Your love doesn't. I am so grateful.

In memoriam
Steve Hayner
(1948–2015),
who joyfully embraced a life
of moving toward the mess.

MOVE TOWARD THE MESS
Published by David C Cook
4050 Lee Vance View
Colorado Springs, CO 80918 U.S.A.

David C Cook Distribution Canada
55 Woodslee Avenue, Paris, Ontario, Canada N3L 3E5

David C Cook U.K., Kingsway Communications
Eastbourne, East Sussex BN23 6NT, England

The graphic circle C logo is a registered trademark of David C Cook.

LCCN 2015953326
ISBN 978-0-7814-1337-4
eISBN 978-0-7814-1429-6

© 2016 John Hambrick
Published in association with the literary agency of The Blythe Daniel
Agency, P.O. Box 64197, Colorado Springs, CO 80962-4197

The Team: Tim Peterson, Keith Wall, Amy Konyndyk, Nick
Lee, Lori Jones, Helen Macdonald, Susan Murdock
Cover Design: Jon Middel
Cover Photo: Thinkstock

Printed in the United States of America
First Edition 2016

1 2 3 4 5 6 7 8 9 10

012616

CONTENTS

FOREWORD

Every once in a while a phrase comes along that covers a lot of territory with just a few words. "Move toward the mess" is one of those phrases. John Hambrick coined it a few years ago. When I heard it, I realized that it captured an essential aspect of the way we do things at North Point Ministries. Our organization has a reputation for being an exciting place. One of the ways we try to sustain that excitement is by encouraging people to practice the lifestyle represented by this deceptively simple little phrase. When we get that right, things happen. There's not much time to be bored.

I'm excited about this book. I'm excited that you have a chance to read it. In the opening chapters you'll discover that this idea of moving toward the mess is based on some of the things Jesus taught in the Gospels. There are six chapters about people and organizations such as Jim Rayburn and Young Life or Patrick Donnelly and Habitat for Humanity, Belfast. They illustrate what can happen when folks get serious about engaging with the messy situations that exist across the street, across town, or across the world. The tactical advice John gives at the end of the book makes moving toward the mess an actionable idea for pretty much everybody. This last part is particularly important. Here's why.

Public opinion polls show that Christians are not highly thought of in our country these days. But if everybody in the American church started to move toward the mess, our nation may start to change its mind about us. They might never believe what we believe, but they'd want us for a neighbor. They'd want to work for us or have us work for them. They'd want their sons and daughters to marry our sons and daughters. The moral and spiritual chaos that seems to dog our country's every step would begin to shrink. People would begin to rethink their views about God and the church. It's happened before. It can happen again.

I hope you find that to be a compelling idea. If so, then reading *Move Toward the Mess* is just what you need to help you plan your next steps. And while it's true that this will chase off the boredom that may hover around the edges of your spiritual life, there's something even more important at stake. We have a chance here to help suffering people. God can use you to make a difference in their lives. If you choose to get involved, God will be honored, people will be helped, and your life will take on a sense of significance that you never thought possible. That's just too good a deal to pass up.

Andy Stanley

ACKNOWLEDGMENTS

It takes a village to raise a child. In this case, the child is a book. There is certainly a village's worth of people to thank. To begin, thanks go to Allison Holley, who, a long time ago, started pointing people toward my phrase "move toward the mess." And thanks to Fred Hadra for some great marketing guidance. Bill and Betsy Duffey, Rodney Anderson, Bill Willits, and Megan Springer were kind enough to read the early versions of several chapters and make helpful comments. Their encouragement was key in moving things along. Additional thanks go to Betsy for suggesting that I attend the Blue Ridge Mountains Christian Writers Conference. That proved to be a pivotal experience. Alton Gansky, Bob Hostetler, and Edie Melson provided some crucial guidance and feedback while I was there.

It was at that conference that I met Blythe Daniel and her wonderful colleague Jessica Kirkland. Blythe is the head of the Blythe Daniel Agency. She is a literary agent extraordinaire and had the courage to take me on board. She has been a phenomenal mentor and guide. Additionally, Blythe knows how to be a pastor to her authors. She, her husband, Art, and their family have become our friends.

I've had the privilege to work with the folks at David C Cook. What an amazing group of people! To Tim Peterson, associate publisher of Trade Books, thanks for taking a chance on a new author. To Tim Close, Lisa Beech, Darren Terpstra, Amy Konyndyk, Annette Brickbealer, Ingrid Beck, Michelle Webb, and Channing Brooks, many thanks for all you're doing to get the word about *Move Toward the Mess* out there. Thanks to Jon Middel for some great cover art. And to Keith Wall, Helen Macdonald, and Lori Jones, a huge thank-you for all your editorial work. You guys are rock stars!

Over at North Point Ministries, my heartfelt thanks goes to Andy Stanley, who agreed to write a foreword, and who has generously quoted me in front of audiences usually the size of small cities.

Then there are my kids, John and Carrell. They have endured countless questions and done more than their share of reading chapters, always with cheerful enthusiasm and helpful feedback. It is such an asset to have people so smart and so culturally attuned in the family!

Last but not least, my heartfelt appreciation goes to my wife, Patty. For the past year or two, she has dropped everything at a moment's notice to read the latest revision of a chapter I was working on. She has read this book in its current and earlier forms multiple times. But most important, a long time ago she decided to move toward the mess. That particular mess happened to be the man she ended up marrying. He is grateful, every day.

INTRODUCTION

Millions long for immortality who don't know what to
do with themselves on a rainy Sunday afternoon.
—Susan Ertz, *Anger in the Sky*

If Jesus had been boring, the Pharisees wouldn't have had him killed. There would have been no crowds. There would have been no controversy surrounding his life. When he said to the disciples, "Follow me," they would have politely declined. The Gospels wouldn't have been written because nobody would have remembered what he said or did. When Jesus talked about his second coming, people would not have been enthusiastic because when you're boring, people don't want you to come back.

But Jesus wasn't boring. He was incredibly engaging. Thousands of people hung on his every word. In his talks, he created tension that set people on edge. He said things that were unexpected. He spoke with authority and courage. Two thousand years later, his words are still reverberating throughout the world.

And it's not just what he said. It's what he did. He did crazy things, things that nobody else had ever done. Ever. These things left people dumbstruck and sometimes scared. "Who then is this, that he commands even wind and water, and they obey him?" (Luke 8:25). If first-century Israel had the communication technology we have today, the evening news would have been constantly filled with the incredible things Jesus did and said. What's remarkable about all of this is that we have a chance to live as Jesus did.

We're not necessarily talking about miracles here. We're talking about living in a way that is engaging, that is memorable, that makes a difference. You and I might never be involved in commanding the wind to stop. But we could be involved in building houses for homeless people to protect them from the wind. We might never raise someone from the dead. But we might be able to help someone's dead marriage come back to life. We might need more than five loaves and two fish to feed people. But we can still feed people in Jesus's name. Figuring out how to live that way is what this book is about.

The reason I feel passionately about this is because my Christian life used to be boring. And that was the problem. It was my "Christian life," separated from the rest of my life, so much so that it was like some sort of useless appendage. It was there, but it didn't have much to do with anything outside itself.

But something happened. God broke through the walls I'd built around my religious life. He did it through a man named Darrell Johnson, the high school pastor at the church I attended after I became a Christian. Darrell started showing up at my school. He came to my games and concerts. He refused to stay inside the church building. He got involved in my messy high school life. In doing so, he modeled for me what Jesus did two thousand years ago and was continuing to do through Darrell.

Jesus gets involved in the chaos of humanity—in all the bad decisions, all the complicated circumstances, all the crazy relationships, all the crises that defy simple answers. He wades right in and hangs around. He doesn't begin by preaching at people. He begins by being with people. At some point along the way, people are so moved by his loving presence that they began to trust him. And when the trust kicks in, lives start to change.

That's what Darrell did for me. Jesus solidified his loving presence in my life through the loving presence of Darrell. I began to realize that's what the Christian life is about—to be nurtured in church but lived out in the world. The walls between my "Christian life" and the rest of my life began to disappear. My whole life got caught up in the loving presence of Jesus. And the message became crystal clear. Jesus did that for me through Darrell. The next step was for Jesus to do that through me for other people. He pretty much dragged me out into the street and told me, "If you want to stop being bored, get involved with what I'm doing out here." My hope is that you will consider starting to live this way.

The thing is, boredom wasn't a problem just for me. It's a pervasive problem for the church in America. In a recent poll conducted by the Barna Research Group, they found that 31 percent of the young adults (ages eighteen to twenty-nine) who left church cite boredom as a significant factor in their decision.[1] And then there are all those others who didn't leave but are still bored. Houston, we do indeed have a problem here.

This is disturbing. How is this even possible? It's like working for Coca-Cola but hating soft drinks. It's like playing baseball but thinking baseball is silly. It just doesn't make sense.

It's tempting to blame it on your church. Yes, maybe your pastor preaches uninspiring sermons. Maybe the music in your church isn't exactly engaging. Maybe the service is too formal or too old-fashioned or too long. Maybe. But that's not really the problem. The problem is the same problem I used to have. The walls I built around my "Christian life" separated it from the rest of my life. The result was a colossal case of boredom. Here's another way to frame things. Think, for a moment, of Christianity as a sport. There's the locker room meeting before the game. And then there's the game. The problem is, we've got the two mixed up. Let me explain what I mean.

In every sport, there is a team meeting before game time. These meetings consist of making sure everybody's on board with the game plan. There's usually an inspirational talk from the coach or manager. Then the team goes out and plays the game. The game is what makes the locker room meeting interesting and relevant. If there were no game, the locker room meeting would be a waste of time. In fact, it would be boring. If there's no game, who cares about game plans? The coach's pep talk would be a stand-alone event without connection to anything outside of the locker room. Since the speech had nothing to do with any particular game, it would be judged solely on the basis of whether or not it was entertaining. Sound familiar?

What about the crowd in the stands? They come expecting to see a game. They're looking forward to displays of skill and courage and sacrifice. They want to see something inspirational. There's something at stake for them out on the field. It somehow has an impact on their lives. They're watching intently to see what happens. They care about who wins.

But what if the team didn't show up on the field? What if the players never left the locker room? The crowd would become angry. They would start to call the players and coaches a bunch of frauds and cowards. The team talks about great things in the locker room, but what if they're afraid to come out on the field and execute the plan? Of course, when we say we're going to do something and fail to do it, we leave ourselves open to being labeled hypocrites. Again, does that sound familiar?

When we Christians start to confuse the locker room with the game, things get boring. How could they not? We talk about love and generosity and grace. Those things come alive and get exciting when they're running loose in the world. But if we only ever talk about those things in church, and never practice them outside the church, things get stale. It might be more comfortable inside the walls of a church, but excitement is found where Jesus is at work—out in the world. That's where he wants us to get involved.

You might find yourself saying, "God wants us to practice love and generosity in the church too." Yes, that's correct. But then he expects us to leverage those loving and generous relationships outside the walls of the church, where love and generosity are sometimes in short supply. People are watching to see if this Christianity business makes any real difference. How can they see that difference if we never get close enough for them to notice?

This book is about getting close enough for people to notice. It's not an indictment of worship services or Bible studies or Sunday school or small groups. On the contrary, those things are immeasurably valuable. Nothing good would happen without them. But from the perspective of the kingdom of God, the church gathers apart from the world so that it may then reenter the world as a witness to Jesus Christ. The game is out there, where things are unpredictable and off script and sometimes overwhelming. When it's all over, nobody's going to ask you how many locker room meetings you attended—they're going to be interested only in what happened out on the field. Admittedly, the game gets very messy. But nobody's bored out there. Nobody.

Part I

PERSPECTIVES AND PROFILES

Chapter 1

CHAIRMAN OF THE BORED NO MORE

There is no such thing on earth as an uninteresting subject;
the only thing that can exist is an uninterested person.
—G. K. Chesterton, *Heretics*

Meet my friend Josh. He's one of those guys. His smile makes you smile. His cheerful spirit is infectious. He can light up a room just by entering it. The last time I saw him, he was on a road trip across the country. His goal was to see sixteen different major league baseball games in sixteen different cities, and he had stopped in Atlanta, where we live, to see the Atlanta Braves. To say that Josh is a baseball fan is a bit of an understatement.

One of the few things that trumps his love for baseball is his love for Jesus Christ. Josh is a passionate Christian, fully engaged and fully committed. But it wasn't always that way. There was a time in his life when his faith wasn't so passionate. Fast cars and loud music excited him. Church did not. The story of his exit from a boring spiritual life is in itself quite interesting. There are several events in his story that represent turning points along the way. One of them happened on a trip he took while in high school.

I was Josh's youth pastor at the time. His boredom wasn't unique—a lot of the people in the high school group were in the same place. I knew that if things didn't change, their lives would assume an all-too-common trajectory: "I grew up in a Christian home but then drifted away from the faith in college." I knew that many of those people never drift back.

I also knew that "shoulding" on people, as Brennan Manning used to say, was a bad idea. For me to get up at the Tuesday night high school group meeting and say, "You shouldn't be bored" wasn't just a waste of time—it was a dangerous strategy. As a speaker, you can use the "should" approach and make people feel guilty, but it doesn't produce passionate followers of Jesus Christ. It merely produces compliant, guilt-driven church people. And once that guilt-based approach to faith gets a hold of you, it's tough to find your way back to grace.

As I continued to think and pray about what I could do for Josh and the rest of the group, I came across an organization called the Center for Student Missions (CSM). This organization took groups of high school kids into South Central Los Angeles for three or four days so they could experience what life there was like. They promised a safe experience. As it turned out, our experience was safe, but in retrospect I wonder if that was due more to God's provision than any organizational expertise on their part.

Our youth group decided to add our own twist to the trip. After our time in South Central, we would drive to Santa Barbara, then sail out to Santa Cruz Island, about thirty miles off the Southern

California coast. The remote location would be the ideal place to reflect on our time in Los Angeles. We called the trip "City to Sea."

So, one Sunday afternoon in July, we loaded four adults and twelve high school kids into cars and made the ninety-minute drive to South Central Los Angeles, where our "headquarters" consisted of two vacant apartments in a sketchy apartment building. We slept on the floor in sleeping bags—the guys in one apartment and the girls in the other. Cockroaches were a bit of a problem.

That first night we adults felt anything but safe. We wondered if we had made a huge mistake, but the CSM staff continued to insist that we were perfectly safe as long as we followed a few rules. Some of the rules seemed ominous, especially the one that read, "Stay away from the windows at night." Why? To decrease the chances of being accidentally shot by a gang member on the street below. Check.

Of course, Josh, who had become enthusiastic about the trip, needed a little reminding. Our first night, around ten o'clock, we had settled into our sleeping bags for the evening when five gunshots rang out on the street below. Josh immediately jumped up and ran to the window to see if he could spot the shooter. I grabbed him and yanked him down. I felt as if I was in some sort of action-adventure movie. We persuaded Josh to stay away from the windows for the remainder of the trip.

Over the next four days, we were immersed in the life of South Central Los Angeles. One day we served at a soup kitchen. Another day we staffed an urban child-care center. We helped sort clothes in a thrift shop. We made sandwiches for homeless people. At night the CSM staff would load us into a couple of vans and take us on tours.

We saw men and women sleeping on the street on LA's infamous "Skid Row." We learned, to our amazement, that it was right around the corner from one of the city's most opulent hotels. We saw people selling cocaine more times than we could count. We saw working girls on the street corners. At times we arrived back at our apartments in silence—we had no words to describe what we felt. The moral and spiritual chaos was palpable.

When it came time to head up to Santa Barbara, we actually felt sad. It's hard to explain, but there was something about choosing to be in the middle of such a painful place that we found compelling. Jesus seemed to be present in a way we just hadn't experienced back at church. The religious boredom that had plagued so many of these students began to disappear. It was being shoved out by a finely balanced sense of purpose and adventure. Lives were being changed, and vocations were being discovered.

The trip out to Santa Cruz Island was beautiful. The weather was gorgeous, and the water a deep blue. At one point we sailed through a school of dolphins. For a minute or two they swam alongside our boats—hundreds of them. We had started to feel at home in the city; we now felt equally at home on the water.

Our days on the island were wonderful, filled with laughter. That was one of the ways we dealt with the stress of our inner-city experience. But we also talked to God and to each other. We discussed our fears, our sense of helplessness, and our growing desire to somehow make a difference. We found a new depth of meaning in the scriptures we studied. We felt as though God's heart for the poor and marginalized, for the destitute and the enslaved, had somehow rubbed off on us. Never again would we think about

South Central as that dangerous place where "those people" live. "Those people" were transformed into fellow human beings who, in a lot of ways, were just like us. They were people God loved and for whom Christ died. In our view, the real tragedy was that very few of them knew that. A week before, very few of us had really cared, but we had changed.

DISPLACING BOREDOM

Josh will tell you that after the trip, church ceased to be boring. It was still the same church, the same worship services, the same sermons, the same everything. But Josh had changed. And as a result, everything started to come alive. At one level, he was still a high school kid who liked to goof around and play video games. But at a deeper level, he had made a transition. He was following Jesus in a new way. That new way led Josh out of the church and into the city—out of the comfort zone and into the chaos zone where things are messy.

Jesus cares about everybody. But he seems to have a particular fondness for those whose need is most obvious. He put it like this:

> Those who are well have no need of a physician, but those who are sick; I have not come to call the righteous, but sinners to repentance. (Luke 5:31–32)

> The harvest is plentiful, but the laborers are few; pray therefore the Lord of the harvest to send out laborers into his harvest. (Matt. 9:37–38)

So … what exactly does Josh's story have to do with you? You are probably not a high school student. But you may be bored. Hopefully, you are beginning to wonder if there is something more to your faith than what you've experienced so far. If that's the case, then Josh's story has everything to do with yours.

For starters, we learned that boredom must be displaced rather than banished. In other words, you can't order boredom to leave. It has to be shoved out by something compelling and engaging, something attractive and meaningful. The City to Sea trip proved to be that kind of experience for Josh. He realized that God was at work in the world and that he could get involved in that work.

A vast sense of opportunity began to open before Josh. He began to see that while he had been sitting bored in church Sunday after Sunday, there were little children who were sitting in abusive homes. There were old folks sitting alone, day after day, in assisted-living facilities. There were young women sitting in cheap hotel rooms, enslaved by human traffickers. There were drug addicts sitting on the street, looking for their next high. And there were legions of homeless people who could sit only in hard and dangerous places.

But it wasn't limited to inner-city problems. There were rich middle-age executives sitting in corporate offices with plenty of money and no meaning in their lives. There were people in every country and continent sitting in their homes on Sunday, never hearing the good news about Jesus Christ. There were people at Buena High School, where most of our students went, who were lonely and hopeless. When all of this started to become clear, Josh just didn't have time to be bored anymore.

The second thing we learn from Josh's story is that our traditional thinking about boredom is wrong. I love the quote by G. K. Chesterton at the beginning of this chapter. It challenges that traditional thinking about boredom and sends the conversation in a surprising direction. It suggests that boredom isn't so much about what's around us as it is about what's inside us. It suggests that the solution to being bored involves a change of heart more than a change of circumstances. It suggests that being bored is more of a choice we make than the result of our situation.

The implications of this are far reaching. For starters, you're not going to conquer this problem by leaving a church that plays organ music on Sunday morning to go to one that uses a rock band. Here's the thing: if boredom is more about your choices than it is about your circumstances, then it won't be long before you'll be bored by *any* kind of church service—if you allow yourself to be. And then you'll start looking for another church, and then another, and then another. At some point you may stop looking altogether. The problem is not the style of your church. It's not the minister or the music. The problem is you and me. Josh didn't solve his boredom problem by changing churches. It was solved when he allowed God to change his heart. It was solved when he moved toward the mess.

DISCUSSION QUESTIONS

1. Do you sense that boredom is prevalent in your church? Why or why not?

2. Has spiritual boredom been a struggle for you? If not, how have you avoided it? If so, why do you think that's the case?

3. Why do you think boredom was not a problem for the Christians we read about in the New Testament?

4. The author suggests that boredom is a choice we make. If that's true, why do people choose to be bored?

5. How would you explain what the author means by the phrase "move toward the mess"?

6. What do you hope will happen in your life as a result of reading this book?

Chapter 2

THE HEART OF THE MATTER

We are saved to serve, not to sit around and wait for heaven.
—Rick Warren, *The Purpose-Driven Life*

Why bother moving toward the mess? It's a great, honest question, and there are a lot of great, honest answers. The story about Josh in the previous chapter makes clear that moving toward the mess can rescue us from boredom and revitalize our faith. If that were the only reason, it would be more than enough. But we're just getting started.

When I follow Jesus out into the world, I meet some amazing people. Like me, they are deeply flawed. But the remarkable thing is this: I learn more about following Jesus from drug addicts and homeless people than practically anyone else. Don't get me wrong—good preaching has its value, and I've learned a lot from some excellent preachers. Still, nothing has moved me into a dependent relationship with Jesus more effectively than facing the moral and spiritual chaos that exists in the world. When that dependency kicks in, the love starts to flow. You start to care about people. They start to get under your skin. That's when the life-change starts. I don't mean just the people on the street—I mean me.

In the 1990s I lived and worked in London, England. My wife, Patty, and I had packed our bags and moved there from Southern California with our two kids, John Jr. and Carrell. I had been working with high school students in both the local church and through the organization Young Life, which we loved doing. But then we had a chance to move to London, and we jumped at it. I was offered a position as associate pastor of the American Church. Shortly thereafter I also became one of the chaplains at King's College London. King's College was right down the street from the Houses of Parliament, and the rarified air of those in positions of influence permeated the campus. They were lovely people and they were definitely upper class. The American Church, however, had a soup kitchen on-site. Its clientele was definitely not upper class. We were on the homeless people's circuit. It was almost as if when people hit the streets of London, someone gave them a road map marked with all the places one could get free food. So we dealt with hungry, homeless folks most every day.

AN UNLIKELY FRIENDSHIP

It was in that context that I met Terry, an Irishman who was about thirty years old. He showed up at the church office one morning around nine o'clock. He had red hair, an angelic face … and he was howling mad. It turns out Terry had started taking Ecstasy the evening before and had spent the night in the steamy club scene of underground London. Somehow, on this particular morning, he found his way to my office as he was crashing, angry that he had no more money for drugs. I learned that he would spend the rest of the day doing who knows what in order to get the money he needed to get high again. This was business as usual for Terry. The only new part was that he began to end his binges in my office.

This first time we met, he announced in an irritated voice that he was gay. It seemed that he expected me to run out of the room screaming. When I calmly replied, "Oh, that's cool," he then proceeded to say, "But I'm not particularly attracted to you." Being a heterosexual, I wasn't sure how to feel about that. I let the remark slide as he continued ranting and raving. He had a lot of pent-up rage. I don't think it was just about the drugs. I think Terry pretty much hated his life—and himself. When he got to my office, it all came out.

Thus began what was to be one of the defining relationships of my time in London. Terry began to come by my office regularly. Sometimes his anger became intense; one time I had to call the police. As they escorted him off the property, he called me a "wanker." The word had little impact on my uninitiated American ears. Later I learned that, within English culture, "wanker" is one of the ultimate profane insults. I didn't see Terry for a while after that. Then one day he showed up again. Neither of us mentioned the previous incident, and soon we got back into the old rhythm. As the weeks went by, we developed a friendship of sorts. I never figured out exactly where he lived because he was rather evasive about that. But if it wasn't on the street, it surely wasn't much better. I wondered how I could help him.

Every once in a while Terry would ask for money. I knew that in England, homeless or near-homeless people could draw a small pension from the government, sort of like welfare in the United States. I knew the drugs he used constantly were expensive. I don't know how he paid for them and still had enough left over to cover the basic expenses of life. So it wasn't surprising to hear him say he needed money for something to eat.

His request created some tension for me. On the one hand, of course we're supposed to help feed hungry people. On the other hand, I worried that instead of buying food he would use the money to buy more Ecstasy. By that time I'd learned that most street people would tell me whatever I wanted to hear if they thought it would get them some cash. I wasn't savvy enough to tell who was lying and who was telling the truth. So it was pointless to look Terry in the eye and ask him if he was really going to use this money for food. That "looking homeless people in the eye" business doesn't really work.

I suspect that sometimes Terry used the money for food and sometimes he used it for drugs. But whether or not that was true, I did notice that he began to appear less haggard and more lucid. He would come around at different times during the day. Our conversations became more civil. He started to think about getting a job and turning his life around.

He never talked about becoming a Christian. It's not that Jesus never came up; it's just that Terry wasn't ready to trust him. Things never seemed to move very far in the direction of faith. I realized that if we could just get him out of the cycle of drug abuse and partying and into some sort of a normal job, it would be a great step forward. Maybe once Terry's life stabilized, he would start to think more seriously about who Jesus was and what that meant.

Then Terry disappeared. There was no warning—he just stopped showing up. There was nothing I could do. There was nobody to call. I prayed, hoping he was at least still alive. And the days passed by.

Finally, several weeks later, Terry showed up again at my office, looking calm and clear. He had decided to swear off the club scene. He'd actually gone out and gotten a job. He was now a conductor on one of London's famous double-decker buses. I was thrilled and told him so. He seemed pleased at my response. I inquired about which route he was on and made it my business to take that bus whenever I could. His life seemed to be moving in a positive direction.

Then Terry disappeared again. And this time he didn't show back up. The man who took his place on the bus knew nothing about him. Nobody in the soup kitchen knew anything about him. I still had no contact details. He was just gone. The weeks stretched into months and the months stretched into years.

Did Terry die? Did he slip back into the club scene? Did he move in with someone and decide to steer clear of "church people," as he called us? Did he head back to Ireland? I never found out. So I don't know if all the hours Terry and I spent talking, arguing, and laughing made any long-lasting difference in his life. But they sure made a long-lasting difference in mine.

God used Terry to clarify what he was calling me to do, what I had essentially been doing all along. It helped me create a category for the people I had been drawn to back in California and some of the experiences I had working there. I thought of the time there was a gang fight at one of our Young Life events. I recalled when my friend Jeff Cowan and I created a venue where high school kids in heavy metal bands could play. By the way, we called it "The Crash Club." And I remembered when another friend, Rick Bundschuh, and I took some out-of-control surf punks on a surfing trip to Baja California. I realized my time with Terry summed up and represented all of these people and all of these efforts. Terry helped me see that God has called me—has called all of us—to move toward the mess. It's just what you do when you're following Jesus.

It's not always easy. I'm not always excited about it. On the contrary, there are days when I'd rather just stay home and watch movies. But moving toward the mess is exactly what God chose to do in Jesus Christ. "For God so loved the world that he gave his only Son, that whoever believes in him should not perish but have eternal life" (John 3:16). The world that God loves, to which he sent his Son, is exactly where the mess is located. And Jesus moved right into the middle of it.

IN THE MIDDLE OF THE MESS

The world thinks religious people spend all their time being, well, religious. Not Jesus. He spent his days with messy people in messy situations. He ate with crooked businessmen who cheated people out of their hard-earned wages. He befriended the terrorists of his day (back then they were called zealots). He hung out with prostitutes—not former prostitutes but girls who were still in the trade. He was constantly in the middle of all manner of messy situations, speaking words of grace and truth and chastising the religious leaders for keeping themselves aloof from these dear people whom God loved. It's what Jesus did back then and what he wants to continue to do now through his people—through you and me.

This doesn't necessarily mean you have to quit your job. It just means you have to think about your job differently. Yes, honor God through the excellence you bring to your work, but realize there's more to it than that. Your job can be a place where you engage with the brokenness of the world. It can provide an opportunity to practice "the transforming power of being with."[1] When you start to open yourself up to this new way of thinking, you'll discover formulas don't work. Religious platitudes will ring hollow. There will be times when you don't know what to do or what to say. The people God brings across your path will care much more about your compassion than your theology. But hang on to your hat because life will start to take on a whole new perspective. It won't be just a job anymore. It will become your calling.

Moving toward the mess isn't an elective for spiritual giants. It's at the center of what God is doing in the world. He moves toward the mess in order to redeem those who have created it. He wants us all to get involved. Granted, we will each have different roles in the effort. It's like being part of a large, multifaceted army. Some soldiers will be on the front lines. Some will be mechanics keeping the tanks and trucks running. And others will be medics taking care of the wounded. You may be in any of a thousand roles as a soldier, but each role is important in fighting the war. Each role contributes to the victory.

So why should you even bother? We mentioned two reasons at the beginning of the chapter: (1) moving toward the mess will kick the boredom right out of your life; (2) it's one of the best ways in the world to learn to follow Jesus. But there's a third reason. Moving toward the mess will soften your heart. You won't experience this until you meet your version of Terry. I'm convinced that God will bring someone like Terry into every Christian's life, including yours, if you let him. When your version of Terry shows up, things get personal. The chaos takes on a human shape. It has a voice. It has a story. You'll discover you're no longer talking about principles and statistics and ideas. You're talking about someone's life, someone you've started to care about. And your heart will start to soften. It might even break. Fortunately, God is in the business of healing broken hearts. And those who have experienced this will tell you that a healed heart beats a hardened heart every time.

Hopefully, you have several questions at this point: *How does this all work? How will we recognize our version of Terry? What do we do then? When should we just listen? When should we say something?* Of course, a lot of these questions can't be answered in advance. The clarity you want will come in the moment as the Spirit leads you. In the meantime, it might be helpful to look at how Jesus handled things when one of his versions of Terry showed up. It happened at a dinner party attended by many important people. The person who showed up was a prostitute. It was awkward, but Jesus handled it masterfully. Keep reading, and in the next chapter, you'll see exactly how he did that.

DISCUSSION QUESTIONS

1. Have you ever served at a soup kitchen? What was it like?

2. Have you ever gotten to know a homeless person? If so, how did that happen? If not, how does the idea of reaching out to someone in need strike you?

3. How do you think having a relationship with a homeless person is different from serving at a soup kitchen?

4. The author said he wasn't sure if his relationship with Terry changed Terry, but he was certain it changed him. What kind of changes do you think he was talking about?

5. Have you ever developed an "unlikely friendship"—a relationship between you and someone very different from yourself? How did the experience change you?

6. Do you think it's possible to follow Jesus without moving toward the mess? Why or why not?

Chapter 3

SIMON'S DINNER PARTY

Once you label me you negate me.
—Søren Kierkegaard

The dinner party described in Luke 7 has to be one of the most awkward social events in the history of the planet. It started with the host, Simon, who was a Pharisee. We don't really have an equivalent category for Pharisees in twenty-first-century Western culture. The best way to think about them is as if they were half archbishop and half US senator. In other words, they were very powerful people in both the political and religious worlds. There were probably a lot of Pharisees at the party that night. So, by cultural standards, for Jesus to be invited to Simon's house was a big deal. But in this case, it was not a gesture of friendship.

When Jesus arrived, Simon did not offer the common courtesies that a good host should have offered. It was a glaring omission, not the kind of thing you'd do by accident. He was obviously making a point, perhaps to remind Jesus of his lowly standing in society. Perhaps Simon felt this was necessary because Jesus had been publicly challenging the Pharisees. Perhaps he thought that by humiliating Jesus he would shut him up.

Under these circumstances, the dinner conversation must have been awkward. If they spoke of anything at all, it must have been about trivial matters. All of a sudden, a woman burst into the room. How she got in is anyone's guess. I suspect she might have had a prior "acquaintance" with one of Simon's servants and called in a favor.

The words used in the text suggest she was a prostitute. Then, as now, when a prostitute showed up at the house of a political or religious leader, there was bound to be a scene, the kind that provoked gasps and whispers among the dinner guests. Once in the room, she made a beeline for Jesus, her tears beginning to flow. She noticed that Jesus's feet were dirty—Simon hadn't given him an opportunity to wash them. So she started to wash Jesus's feet using a mixture of tears and perfume. When she finished, she couldn't find a towel. So she used her hair to wipe them clean. This just keeps getting more and more awkward.

CONVENTIONAL WISDOM TURNED UPSIDE DOWN

Had I been the recipient of this kind of attention by that kind of woman in such a proper setting, I would have immediately stood up and said, "Simon, I've never seen this woman before." I would have then proceeded to distance myself from her—literally and figuratively—to ensure that nobody got any ideas about the nature of our relationship, even though there was no relationship. I suspect you might have done the same thing. But not Jesus.

After this display of emotion, the room must have gone completely silent. Without missing a beat, Jesus took charge of the situation and transformed a terribly awkward situation into an exceedingly profound moment. He told a brief but poignant parable about a loan shark and two people who owed him money. One man owed a lot, the other a little. The loan shark decided to forgive them both. Jesus then posed a question. "Now which of them will love him more?" (v. 42). In a voice probably dripping with condescension, Simon answered, "The one, I suppose, to whom he forgave more" (v. 43).

Jesus then asked another question, this one directed at the host: "Turning toward the woman he said to Simon, 'Do you see this woman?'" (v. 44). At one level the answer was obvious. Of course Simon saw the woman. All eyes in the room had been riveted on her for the past ten minutes. But that wasn't what Jesus meant. Jesus asked if Simon saw her desperation, her sorrow, her appeal for grace and forgiveness. And the answer was just as obvious. No, Simon had not seen this. All he had seen was a scandal unfold in his own dining room, confirming his low opinion of Jesus.

Jesus then proceeded to point out how shamefully Simon had treated him, listing all the common courtesies Simon had withheld upon his arrival. He contrasted that with the utterly loving way he was treated by the woman. Completing the contrast, he said, "Therefore I tell you, her sins, which are many, are forgiven, for she loved much; but he who is forgiven little, loves little" (v. 47). In a matter of seconds, Jesus turned the dinner party upside down. He completely reoriented everybody and everything. Simon, who began the evening as the powerful and holy religious figure, was defrocked. He was revealed to be the arrogant and ungrateful person he really was behind all the spiritual pageantry. The woman, on the other hand, was elevated. Jesus revealed her to be a grateful and loving daughter of the Most High God. Her passionate intrusion was instantly legitimized.

This was all accomplished in a flash, as Jesus assumed his proper role—the Lord, the giver of grace. The woman, who was forgiven much, loved much. Simon, who was forgiven little, loved little. But both were dependent on forgiveness. God's grace is the great leveler of humankind. Simon must have been furious to hear Jesus suggest that at best he was only this woman's equal, but more likely her inferior. To drive the point home, Jesus turned to the woman and said something no mere human has the right to say: "Your sins are forgiven" (v. 48).

This statement was absolutely scandalous from a Pharisee's point of view. No one had the right to absolve people from their sins but God alone. Unless Jesus was God (a point Simon was totally unwilling to consider), he had just added blasphemy to the sins he had already committed that evening. I'm surprised that Simon didn't rush across the room and try to strangle Jesus there and then. Be that as it may, it's likely that after the dinner party, Simon joined the group of people who began to plot Jesus's death.

MESSY PEOPLE WILL FIND YOU

What can we learn from this incident at Simon's house? Keep in mind the story in chapter 2 about Terry. How will this prepare you for the day when you meet your version of Terry? To begin with, you can relax a little bit. You probably won't have to look for your Terry. Chances are, he will find you.

Here's the thing. Once you put yourself out there, people will start to notice. Many will keep their distance. They aren't ready to change. They are comfortable where they are and they're not ready to trust some sort of "church person" who has shown up in their midst. It's no good trying to get people to change when they aren't ready. So love them however you can, with no strings attached. But don't chase after them. Your version of Terry will be the person who moves in your direction.

Second, it's possible that you'll receive negative feedback from some of the religious folks in your life. This might be motivated by genuine concern for you on their part. They may worry that you're missing some church functions because you're spending time with "that person." They may wonder if it's a good idea for you to be seen with him or her in public. My boss, Andy Stanley, points out that Jesus never worried about guilt by association. Neither should you.

Finally, always lead with grace. Jesus didn't lecture the woman about the need to change her ways. He didn't shame her, didn't evaluate her, and didn't give her a plan for getting off the street. He started by forgiving her. This doesn't mean that you never encourage your version of Terry to consider a new lifestyle. It just means that's not where you start.

That said, you might still feel a strong urge to start with life-change and then get to grace. You might even feel guilty about not critiquing the details of the way he or she lives. But don't give in! If you lead with grace, you are likely to get around to lifestyle issues someday. If you lead with "change your ways," not only will you never get to grace, but you won't get to see the person change his or her life either. Your potential Terry will write you off as another judgmental Christian and walk away. Believe me, I learned this the hard way.

When I was a new Christian, I was one part enthusiasm and two parts defensiveness. I came out of a permissive counterculture anchored by rock music and drugs. When I started to follow Christ, my friends did not respond positively. They all thought I had done something incomprehensible and made no bones telling me about it.

However, every once in a while, when nobody else was around, they would come by my house, one at a time. They didn't want to be seen with me in public. But they were curious about my newfound faith. It was a golden opportunity for me to love them right where they were with no judgment. But what did I do? I started in on the evils of their sinful ways. What did they do? They left. My behavior only confirmed their suspicions that Christians were a bunch of self-righteous hypocrites. It took me a long time to realize that grace was more important than my observations about someone else's life.

That's a painful story for me to tell. But the story in the next chapter is a joyful one. It's about my friends Leroy and Janelle Lamar. It also involves a prostitute. Actually, it involves several prostitutes. But fortunately, Leroy and Janelle responded to these women as Jesus would have. As a result, what's happening is nothing short of amazing.

DISCUSSION QUESTIONS

1. Have you ever met someone like Simon? Without mentioning names, what were the circumstances through which you met?

2. Why was Simon so arrogant?

3. Does your church or faith community encourage meeting messy people? Why or why not?

4. Is there a "Terry" in your life? How did you meet? How are things going? If there isn't a Terry in your life right now, how do you feel about finding one or letting him or her find you?

5. Is it easy or hard for you to lead with grace? Explain your answer.

6. How do you know when it's time to talk about life-change with somconc?

Chapter 4

HOT DOGS AND PRAYERS

If we don't heal our own 'hood, who will?

—Nelly

Every city has places where the veneer of "things are fine" has worn so thin that it's become transparent. Things are not so fine, and the people aren't doing so well. The streets do have names (with apologies to U2), but those names carry baggage. The rest of the city knows them. When these names are mentioned, there's always a knowing reply: "Yeah, I've heard about that area. I try to avoid it." But then there are people like Leroy and Janelle Lamar. "That area" is where they live. They decided to stay and try to make a difference.

Leroy and Janelle are the kind of people you'd like to spend time with. Leroy is well read and easygoing. He is finishing his master's degree in philosophy but is so down-to-earth that he doesn't come across as heady or supersophisticated. Janelle has a gentle fire about her; she is passionate and focused but not in an off-putting way.

In December 2005 the Lamars moved to the Capitol View neighborhood of Atlanta. Capitol View is one of "those areas." It's filled with older homes. Some of them have been fixed up and are

47

quite charming. Others have been abandoned by their owners and are used by various people to ply their trades. It seems as though there is a small, independently owned market on every other street corner. Inside they sell food and sundries. Outside the men standing around sell crack. And the girls who walk by are quite often selling themselves.

Leroy and Janelle originally moved into this neighborhood for the same reasons most people move into a neighborhood—there was a house they could afford in a convenient part of town. Leroy was finishing his degree and Janelle was pursuing her career. There was no nonprofit that offered them a job. They were not part of a neighborhood organization committed to changing things. There was just Capitol View, with all its baggage. Originally, they were just like everybody else—they wanted the police to arrest all the criminals and lock them all away. Then something happened.

LIFE AT THE INTERSECTION

Around the corner from their home is the intersection of Desoto and Genessee Streets. It seems to be representative of the neighborhood as a whole. There are three houses and a vacant lot. The blue house is a crack house. The brown house is a brothel. The gray house is a halfway house for addicts. Leroy jokes that if you want to try to get off crack, all you have to do is walk across the street. Most people would look at this intersection and walk the other way. That's what Leroy and Janelle did initially. But they were also friends with Peter and Jessica Gross, another Christian couple who lived in the neighborhood. Peter and Jessica saw an opportunity.

In 2006 Peter and Jessica started something called "Hot Dogs and Prayers." Peter saw it as a chance to establish a redemptive presence in the neighborhood. They decided to set up a little stand at the corner of Desoto and Genessee. They would give away hot dogs and ask how they could pray for people. There was no big plan with five next steps. They didn't have any tracts to pass out. They didn't have any buses waiting to whisk people away to some church. They just had hot dogs and prayers. That was it. They asked Leroy and Janelle to join them.

The two couples were at the intersection every Sunday evening at five. They stayed until the hot dogs ran out—and the neighborhood showed up. Drug dealers and addicts. Prostitutes and their customers. Families with little kids. Old folks who had seen better times in the neighborhood. They all came. Through these encounters, something important happened. Leroy and Janelle got to know their neighbors and their neighbors got to know them. Slowly, as the weeks went by, they began to hear peoples' stories. Leroy's and Janelle's hearts began to change. They became less interested in locking up the bad guys and more interested in getting to know the bad guys, the same way Jesus did in the New Testament. They found one type of story to be common and particularly poignant. It was the story told by most of the girls who worked as prostitutes on the streets of Capitol View. They found one person's story particularly poignant. Her name was Rita.[1]

Rita's mom was a prostitute. When her mother wasn't working, she was smoking crack in one of the many crack houses in the neighborhood. So as a little girl, instead of going to school, Rita spent her days wandering around the streets of Capitol View by herself. A family friend saw this and began to take an interest. Rita ended up moving in with this family. What should have been a blessing turned into a curse, since the men in the family began sexually abusing Rita, who was just nine years old.

As Rita grew older, she began to search for some kind of love outside of the home where she was being abused. Everything she had experienced told her that she was worthless except as a sexual object. So that's the direction her search took her. She started dancing in strip clubs along Fulton Industrial Boulevard when she was in ninth grade. The pimps who worked the area around the club took notice. They persuaded Rita to begin work as a prostitute. They took everything from her. She had no self-esteem. Her body belonged to whoever had the money and the time. It's no surprise that, in order to deal with the pain, Rita started to self-medicate. Alcohol became her drug of choice. By the time she was nineteen, she was drinking whatever cash the pimps allowed her to keep.

As the years passed, Rita began to lose her youthful good looks. She became less and less physically appealing. At some point, the pimps decided she was all used up. They drove her back to Capitol View, dumped her out onto the street, and told her to stay there. So Rita ended up back where she started, addicted and alone. She had lost the only thing that had ever made her life valuable to anybody. Well, almost.

While Rita may have no longer had the looks needed to work the clubs and streets along Fulton Industrial Boulevard, she could still eke out a living turning tricks in Capitol View and Pittsburgh, the neighborhood just up the road. The men there weren't as picky. But the money wasn't as good either, and there were no pimps around to protect their investment. Rita was standing on the bottom rung of the sex trade industry. And then, one Sunday afternoon, she saw some people giving away hot dogs at the corner of Desoto and Genessee.

She was immediately struck by the fact that these people didn't want anything from her. On top of that, they were actually interested in her, not as a body but as a human being. It was unlike anything she had ever experienced. She became a regular. And every time she showed up, Leroy and Janelle and Jessica and Peter loved her, valued her, and expressed concern about her well-being. There was no judgment, only concern. It wasn't long before Rita began to come by Leroy and Janelle's house during the week. As time went on, Rita still worked the streets but also became part of the Lamar household.

Then Janelle became pregnant. The doctor told the couple she would give birth to twins. Rita was certain that would bring their friendship to an end. What young couple wants an over-the-hill prostitute around when there are about to be babies in the house? But, even as Janelle got visibly more pregnant, they continued to welcome Rita with open arms. Finally, their love wore Rita down. She started to seriously consider leaving the streets, but she had nowhere to go. The handful of local nonprofits that provided residence for women trying to escape the sex trades were full.

So Leroy and Janelle did something as unthinkable as it was unavoidable. They invited Rita to live with them. On Christmas Day 2011, Rita moved in. She would stay until a space opened up at one of the residence programs. The Lamar household was changed forever.

TRANSFORMATION TAKES TIME

Life with Rita was messy. There would be two steps forward, then one step back. A life formed by sexual abuse, prostitution, and drug addiction doesn't change overnight. Leroy and Janelle had no formal training in assisting a woman with this background. Living with a prostitute trying to get off the street created a steep learning curve. But they were determined to love Rita. And little by little, they began to see progress. Finally, on Valentine's Day 2012, a space for Rita opened up at Wellspring Living, a residential rehab program for sex workers. But the story was just getting started.

At a certain point in the program at Wellspring, Rita was allowed to leave the facility for the weekend. She would come and stay with Leroy and Janelle. But the Lamars' life had changed. Janelle had given birth to twin boys, Loxley and Leroy IV. While Loxley was the picture of health, Leroy IV was diagnosed with Down syndrome. As a result, the family's life became significantly more complicated. In the months ahead, they faced a variety of health problems that were stressful and time consuming, not to mention scary. But the Lamars continued to make room in their lives for Rita.

One Friday, as Leroy drove Rita up to the house for a weekend visit, they saw a prostitute Rita recognized. It was an old friend named Paris. They exchanged greetings, and then Paris disappeared up the street. Later that evening, Rita started to worry about Paris. She asked Leroy to go find her. So Leroy got in his car and started searching, finally finding Paris working the street in a neighborhood just north of Capitol View. That was the beginning of a long and ultimately life-changing relationship. Like Rita, Paris was surprised that these people seemed to care about her with no strings attached. But unlike Rita, Paris was prone to talk about it with the girls in the neighborhood. It was obvious that God was using Leroy and Janelle to change Paris's life. But he was also using Paris to change theirs.

Paris was born in Atlanta. While she has a lot of good things to say about her mom, she never talks about her dad. Married young, Paris had her first child, a son, when she was eighteen. Things were fairly normal for a few years, but something stirred inside Paris, something that disrupted her marriage and began to dismantle her life. It almost killed her.

Paris decided to move out, leaving her son behind. She had to make a living, so she started to dance in a strip club called the Blue Flame Lounge in the Fulton Industrial Boulevard area. At first, the tips she received were in the form of cash. But as a more sinister element began to frequent the club (Paris refers to these men as "the boys from Miami"), the tips began to come in the form of little packets of cocaine. As is so often the case, things progressed from bad to worse. Her dancing morphed into prostitution, and her cocaine tips launched her into addiction. She began to party with anyone who would help her get high.

It turns out, there were a lot of men who were willing to do that, including some high-profile NBA players and the occasional Atlanta police officer. Paris recalls one cop who would have her get in his car and put on his uniform jacket so Paris would look like another cop. They would drive somewhere and have sex. The officer would then pay her and drive her back to the club.

For a while, Paris's life looked like some sort of steamy Hollywood movie. She was partying with the big boys, who made sure she had all the coke she needed. But years of this started to erode her good looks, even at the early age of twenty-five. As her cocaine use morphed into smoking crack, her social skills began to evaporate as well. Soon, the party was over. Like Rita, she wound up back on the streets of Capitol View, alone and addicted.

When Leroy found her, she was in bad shape. After their work with Rita, he and Janelle knew there was no easy turnaround, so, once again, they settled in for the long haul. They were committed to loving Paris as they had loved Rita. There were the same seemingly endless series of ups and downs, the same days filled with hope followed by the same days filled with disappointment. But once again, unconditional love began to have its effect. Paris started to change—very slowly at first, but soon the progress became obvious.

In the meantime, Paris started to talk about Leroy and Janelle with the girls on the street. She told them about this couple who would help, who would love without judgment. She started passing around Leroy's phone number, and eventually the girls started to call. What had started as an expression of Christ's love for Rita and Paris blossomed into a full-time street ministry to prostitutes.

As the number of hours needed to care for these women began to escalate, Leroy and Janelle realized they needed help. Janelle needed to keep her sales job to pay the bills. But all of Leroy's other activities began to disappear. Caring for the girls became a full-time job for him. All of this, on top of taking care of the twins. Their search for help became urgent.

SEEKING HELP, FINDING GRACE

Try as they might, no help appeared. There were small churches scattered throughout the neighborhood, but they had their own battles to fight and just couldn't spare the time or money.

At the beginning of 2012, their friend Aaron Fortner made a suggestion. Why not start their own nonprofit, which would give them a vehicle for raising funds and provide a tax-deductible opportunity for their donors? It could provide an identity for the community. And once it was up and running, Leroy could draw a salary. It just so happened that, shortly after Aaron's suggestion, a gathering called Plywood Presents was forming to equip people interested in local, socially innovative nonprofits. It was just what Leroy and Janelle needed, so they signed up immediately.

At the event, they met Jeff Shinabarger, creator of Plywood Presents and its parent organization, Plywood People. They also met Bob Goff, author of the amazing book *Love Does*. They were coached by Jeff and encouraged by Bob. As a result, in April of 2012, Serenity's Steps was born. Leroy and Janelle now had an organization that gave visibility to their work, and provided them with financial help.

Leroy and Janelle realized that it was one thing to get the girls off the street; it was quite another to get them plugged into another way of making a living. For the most part, these were broken human beings with rock-bottom self-esteem. They had no job skills. They had no understanding of a workplace culture. Being on time, dressing appropriately, submitting to the authority of a boss, mutual cooperation, and treating others with respect were not things that came easily to them. Leroy would find them minimum-wage jobs out in the community, but the girls just didn't have what it took and often ended up getting fired. If they couldn't find jobs, they would just end up back on the street. It was the only "job" they knew. Leroy and Janelle needed to help them find something else.

In the summer of 2013, Leroy and Janelle visited Thistle Farms in Nashville, Tennessee. Thistle Farms is a community of women who have survived prostitution, trafficking, and addiction. Their lives are slowly being changed by the love they find there. One way that love is expressed is through "social enterprise," another name for vocational training. Thistle Farms employs women to make a variety of body-care and paper products to sell, and provides a supportive workplace where they learn the skills necessary to earn a living wage. Once again, it was exactly what Leroy and Janelle needed to see.

Making paper products such as journals, thank-you cards, and wedding invitations struck Leroy and Janelle as a perfect solution to their problem, given the low start-up costs, manageable skill development, and strong earning potential. On top of it all, there was a metaphor embedded in this particular social enterprise. To quote the website they would soon create:

> Our product itself speaks to the healing and repurposing of each woman's life—we craft handmade paper out of used, seemingly unwanted scraps of paper and showcase it in beautiful journals, cards and stationery.[2]

In October of 2013, "That Grace Restored," a vocational development program, was officially launched at Serenity's Steps. While it started slowly, as most new businesses do, it picked up speed. The small operation was originally located in Leroy and Janelle's home but has recently leased work space that will allow for expansion. Not only do the girls learn the process of making paper products, but they are also given training in social and personal skills so they can obtain and keep jobs in the community.

Serenity's Steps and its accompanying social enterprise, That Grace Restored, have continued to broaden their outreach. As of this writing, they are involved with thirty-five women and four men. The Lamars will tell you that progress has been slow and uneven. At times disaster strikes. In June of 2014, Coco, a transgender male prostitute, was murdered just down the road from where Leroy and Janelle live. But through it all, one thing is clear: Leroy and Janelle are called to love these men and women. It is the particular mess Jesus has called them to move toward. And through them he is bringing life and redemption to those who previously had no hope. It's what the kingdom of God is doing in Capitol View. It's what the kingdom of God is doing in your neighborhood. It's what the kingdom of God does everywhere.

To learn more about Serenity's Steps and That Grace Restored, visit the website www.serenityssteps.org.

DISCUSSION QUESTIONS

1. What experience have you had with a neighborhood like Capitol View?

2. What do you think about the "hot dogs and prayers" idea? Have you heard of, or been involved in, similar outreaches?

3. What did you find particularly disturbing about Rita's story?

4. How is Paris's story different from Rita's? How is it the same?

5. What impresses you most about Leroy and Janelle?

6. Are there any opportunities you're interested in exploring as a result of hearing about Serenity's Steps?

Chapter 5

YOU ARE HERE

The church is not a country club for saints. It's a hospital for sinners.
—Anonymous

Let the above words sink in for a moment. When we understand what the church is, it makes our presence in the world engaging and effective. When we misunderstand the nature of the church, we tend to do more harm than good. Interestingly enough, the "dinner parties" described in the preceding two chapters make this point loud and clear.

In chapter 3, we read about a dinner party thrown by Simon the Pharisee. It happened in a very distinguished setting. Simon likely served a very impressive meal. In chapter 4, we read about the dinner party thrown by Leroy and Janelle Lamar. It happened on a street corner in the bad part of town. Leroy and Janelle served hot dogs. While a prostitute crashed Simon's dinner party, the Lamars' dinner party was actually thrown for prostitutes. Clearly, there are two different agendas operating here. And the people behind those agendas thought about themselves and their respective faith communities in two different ways.

This brings us back to the quote at the beginning of the chapter. If you think your church is a country club for saints, then it follows that (a) by default you consider yourself a saint, and (b) you will discourage messy/sinful people from coming because the church is not for them. If you think your church is a hospital for sinners, then (a) by default you consider yourself a sinner, and (b) messy/sinful people are welcome because that's who the church is for. Because he thought he was a saint, Simon considered prostitutes to be sinners and therefore fundamentally different from him. Leroy and Janelle, on the other hand, think prostitutes are fundamentally the same as they are because *everyone* is a sinner. So why wouldn't you reach out to them? That's who the church is for. We're all in the same boat. We all need saving. Leroy and Janelle would say the only difference between them and the prostitutes is that they are trusting Jesus to save them. In the sense that we're using the word here, there is no such thing as a saint.

I gained additional clarity on this issue the other day when I dropped by that vast repository of spiritual insights—our local shopping mall. I went to check out a new store that had recently opened. I didn't know where it was located, so I found one of those displays with several maps on it, one map for each section and level of this huge retail extravaganza. But there was a problem. Somebody had peeled off the red dot that says, "You are here." As a result, it took me forever to figure out how to get to this new store. It turns out that it's really important to know your starting point in order to arrive at your destination.

Let's say you're looking at another kind of map, a map that displays spiritual realities. On this map, there's a big red circle. This circle represents the mess, the sinful turbulence that plagues all of humanity. The crucial question is, Where should we put the dot that says, "You are here"? Simon would place his dot well above the circle. Janelle and Leroy would place their dot *inside* the circle. That's who the church is for—people inside the circle, people in the mess.

WE'RE ALL IN THE MESS TOGETHER

We Christians are in the mess. This is vitally important. Not much good will happen when we move toward the mess if we don't get this right. We don't need to drive across town to find it. We don't need to visit our unchurched neighbors across the street to encounter it. We need only look at our own hearts, our own families, our own lives. If we decide to follow Jesus, the first mess we will encounter is our own.

Of course, the messy details will differ from person to person. Some things are illegal and others are not. Some things have a moral stigma about them, while others are winked at by our culture. What they all have in common is the potential to twist and warp the human spirit. Some work more quickly than others, but they all eventually consume us.

In one person's case, the struggle might be with crack. In another case, the struggle is with anger. Some struggle with alcohol. Others struggle with envy. Some are murderers. Others are gossips. Some are addicted to heroin. Others are addicted to using credit cards. One person might self-medicate with promiscuous sexuality. The other uses ice cream. Some people are violent. Others are mean spirited—they have never touched another person in anger, but their tongues cause more pain than any punch ever would. The apostle Paul, in his famous letter to the church in Rome, puts it this way: "All have sinned and fall short of the glory of God" (Rom. 3:23).

So the truth is, we don't reach out to addicts as people who are completely free of addiction. We don't attempt to help the poor as people free from financial struggles. We don't reach out to the lonely as people who never feel alone. We don't share the gospel as people who have allowed the gospel to conquer every sin in our lives. We don't reach out to messy people as people who have their lives all together. Yes, we are gradually being changed by God's love. But often the process is agonizingly slow. And we don't like that.

As I thought about this, I remembered attending an evening worship service at a church down the street. The pastor decided to preach on the pervasive problem of sexual lust. Toward the end of the message, the minister gave people a chance to pray about this problem. Realizing the particularly shameful nature of this struggle, he didn't ask people to come to the front of the sanctuary. He led people in a prayer they could say silently while remaining in their seats. Right after the prayer, a gentleman sitting in front of me exclaimed, "I've been healed of the demon of lust!" I didn't know this guy, but on the basis of stories of hundreds of men that I do know, here's what I think was going on inside that gentleman's head: This struggle was embarrassing for him. It caused him a great deal of distress. Understandably, he was looking for a quick fix, something that would make the problem go away. He was tired of the struggle and wanted some sort of spiritual pill that he could "take" to make it stop. We are all like that. We would all like to figure out how to make our struggles go away quickly.

But that's not the way sin works. Ask anyone in a twelve-step program. Those folks will tell you that once an alcoholic, always an alcoholic. That's why they start each meeting introducing themselves by saying, for example, "My name is Bill, and I'm an alcoholic." That doesn't necessarily mean they're still drinking. It just means they're still working on getting or staying sober. They will tell you there is no quick fix, no spiritual pill to "make it go away." They say that healing is a lifelong process, and that fits well with what Scripture has to say about sin. If there were some sort of magical prayer you could say to make sin go away, there would be no need for the warnings and words of encouragement we find laced throughout the New Testament. All we would need to do is say the magic prayer.

So the guy who was "healed of the demon of lust" walked out of that service feeling almost euphoric. But I suspect that the next day or week or month, he was back to his old troubles. It would be the same if he had struggled with gambling or lying or any of the hundreds of dysfunctional things that plague human beings. Was there a demon involved? It's possible, but I doubt it. Did the prayer help? Definitely! But did the problem go away permanently? I don't think so. That's usually not the way it works.

Out-of-control appetites need a resilient, pervasive commitment to self-control. Acquiring self-control is like developing muscles—and they don't bulk up overnight. They grow slowly. Self-control requires ongoing prayer, an intentional plan, and a consistent, Spirit-empowered effort to grow. But the thing that fuels this process—that provides the energy needed for the process to work—is grace. Without being infused by God's grace, this whole life-change thing doesn't work. It runs out of gas.

Grace is the good news, the great news, the "Holy cow, I can't believe this!" news for all of us. We have been forgiven. God is no longer keeping score. Christ's death and resurrection took care of all of that. We have been pardoned. We are free. When this sinks in, peace begins to pour into our souls. We experience a sense of relief. God is bigger than the mess. And that confidence enables us to invest in things like acquiring self-control. It's not so we can earn God's favor. It's because we already have it.

GRACE NEEDED AND FREELY GIVEN

If you want to read a poignant example of someone who has experienced the relief of grace, check out Romans 7 and 8. It's a classic, eloquent, breathtaking account of the apostle Paul's struggle and how he finds peace as the struggle continues. In Romans 7, he talks about the sin in his life. It's a painful revelation written in the present tense. This means he's not talking about his life before he was a Christian. He's not talking about his life when he was a new Christian. He is talking about his current reality—a very messy reality.

This is astounding. The guy who wrote half the New Testament locates his life inside the red circle, just like Leroy and Janelle. He is in the mess. This bothers him so much that, toward the end of the chapter, he screams out, "Wretched man that I am! Who will deliver me from this body of death?" (Rom. 7:24).

Now don't miss this next part. First of all, pay close attention to what Paul doesn't say about his struggles. He doesn't say, "So I realized I just need to work harder." He doesn't say, "So I prayed this prayer and the struggle went away." He doesn't say, "I realize my struggles aren't as serious as those of the people in the bad part of town. So I don't think I'm really in the red circle. At least not in the way they are."

What he does say is this: "There is therefore now no condemnation for those who are in Christ Jesus" (Rom. 8:1). The solution to Paul's problem is grace. Not self-effort. Not a spiritual "pill" that can make the struggles go away. Not deciding that you're better than most people. What gives Paul peace in the middle of the mess is God's outrageous, unconditional forgiveness.

Paul's solution is drastically different from the solution of Simon the Pharisee, who didn't think he needed grace. Paul and Leroy and Janelle see God's grace as a present reality while they are in the mess. They have placed their "You are here" sticker squarely in the middle of the red circle, and God is meeting them right where they are.

Paul puts it this way: "But God shows his love for us in that while we were yet sinners Christ died for us" (Rom. 5:8). That is the gospel. That is good news. That is grace. And so even in the middle of the mess, we can breathe a sigh of relief. God has got this messy situation covered. There is hope. We've been rescued.

Now about those dinner parties … Just for a second, think of them as "The Parable of the Two Dinner Parties." You can use this parable to see how you're doing with this idea of moving toward the mess. Here's the question: Is your life more like Simon's dinner party or more like the Lamars' dinner party?

First of all, where are your parties being held? Look back over the past month or so. Can you recall intentionally spending some time in some messy places, maybe some places outside your comfort zone? Maybe it was a soup kitchen. Maybe it was your neighbor's house. Maybe it was at the bar with your softball team. Simon avoided messy places. Leroy and Janelle sought them out.

Then what happened? Simon humiliated people. The Lamars served people. And notice Leroy and Janelle didn't move too fast. They didn't expect anything from the people they met. They didn't feel compelled to preach the gospel on that street corner. They started by just handing out hot dogs and asking people how they could pray for them. That was brilliant. They put themselves out there in a distinctively Christlike way without freaking people out.

So that's what you have to figure out when you go to the bar with your softball team. How can you be a distinctively Christlike presence without freaking people out? That's the crazy thing about Jesus. People flocked to him. He often couldn't get from one place to another because of the crowds. It's interesting that his followers, two thousand years later, often seem to have the opposite effect. It's no good going to the bar with your softball team if you're going to make everybody feel awkward. The only people who seemed to feel awkward around Jesus were people like Simon. So the dinner parties we throw need to be places where messy people feel safe and welcome.

This brings us to the third point of our parable. You can tell how your dinner parties are doing by who shows up. You will know that you have connected with messy people if they arrive in your life. If you have created a Christlike presence that is welcoming and safe for messy people, they will come. If the only people who come to your parties are the Simons of the world, then that should tell you something.

Of course it's safer to throw dinner parties for church people. That's what Simon did. We know how they think. They're probably not going to do or say things that make us uncomfortable. They're probably not going to do things with which we disagree. After a dinner party attended by church people, we will feel things went well. Everything was predictable. Everything went according to plan. If messy people show up, the chaos factor goes up. So maybe you'll know you're throwing parties like the Lamars' when you finish the evening wondering what on earth just happened.

At the risk of being obvious, we can summarize the main point of the "Parable of the Two Dinner Parties" by saying that working with messy people is messy. Simon refused to take that on. Leroy and Janelle embraced it. We can't stay in our comfort zones and meaningfully connect with messy people. We're going to be off balance. We will struggle with what to say and whether to say it. We will wonder if we are compromising. We'll wonder if we have been too religious or if we have not been Christlike enough. There are not many guidelines to follow out there in the mess. It's not formulaic. What worked in one situation won't work in the next. We'll have to rely on the Spirit's prompting, all the time remembering that we are in the mess along with these messy people. But there is one thing you won't have to worry about while following Jesus into the chaos of the world—boredom. You won't even come close to it.

Before we move on to looking at a very messy situation in Belfast, Northern Ireland, I want to refer again to that diagram we mentioned earlier. It's the one with the big red circle that represents the moral and spiritual chaos that has engulfed humanity. I hope you have placed your "You are here" sticker inside the red circle, along with the apostle Paul and the Lamars. There's one more sticker to place on the diagram. It's the one we would use to represent Jesus. If we created such a sticker, where should it go? After all, he's the one person who isn't messy. He's the only one who could appropriately be placed well outside the circle. Which makes the place where he shows up all the more surprising. If you look carefully, you'll notice he's not outside the circle. He's there right next to you . . . in the middle of the mess.

DISCUSSION QUESTIONS

1. What do you think of the quote at the beginning of the chapter? Is it a new thought, a confirmation of what you believe, or something with which you disagree?

2. Referring to the diagram with the big red circle representing the mess, where do you think most church people would put their "You are here" sticker? What about most unchurched people? What's the thinking behind your answer?

3. In the list of things we struggle with, both drugs and envy are mentioned. The dangers of drugs are obvious. How is envy spiritually dangerous?

4. Do you think most people would be surprised by the apostle Paul's struggle with sin as it's recounted in Romans 7? Why or why not?

5. Why do so many people attempt to address their sinful struggles with something other than God's grace?

6. What might be a next step for people who want to make some changes in their lives as a result of reading this chapter?

Chapter 6

BUILDING IN BELFAST

It is a symbol of Irish art. The cracked looking-glass of a servant.
—James Joyce, *Ulysses*

This is a story about a man we'll call Patrick Donnelly. It's better if we don't use his real name. You'll see why in just a minute. He is one of the most cheerfully unforgettable people I've ever met. I haven't been able to find him for a long time. I hope he's okay.

I first met Patrick in 1994 on a construction site in the Lower Falls area of Belfast, Northern Ireland. Habitat for Humanity had recently started a branch there, selecting the Lower Falls for their first construction project because of the community's need for decent and affordable housing. The Lower Falls area of Belfast was also a stronghold of the Irish Republican Army, or the IRA.

In short, the IRA has a long, complicated, and often violent history. It is the paramilitary arm of Sinn Féin, the political party of those who favor Northern Ireland's independence from Britain. In 1997, when Sinn Féin was admitted to the Northern Ireland Peace Talks, the IRA committed to a cease-fire. It endorsed the Good Friday Agreement of 1998. This piece of legislation was a major step forward in the troubled relationship between Northern Ireland and Britain. Finally, in 2005, the IRA disarmed.

However, when I met Patrick in 1994, the IRA was still a violent organization. Habitat for Humanity had not chosen the Lower Falls area of Belfast solely because of its housing needs—it hoped to provide a place where peaceful relationships could be developed between the largely Catholic Irish nationalists, from whose ranks the IRA recruited its members, and the largely Protestant Irish loyalists, who wanted to keep Northern Ireland a part of Britain's United Kingdom.

The loyalists had their own paramilitary groups, the largest of which was called the Ulster Defence Association, or the UDA. Their members sometimes referred to themselves as the Ulster Freedom Fighters. The UDA was basically a network of vigilante groups founded in 1971. They were committed to armed opposition against the IRA. Another prominent loyalist paramilitary group was called the Ulster Volunteer Force, or the UVF, which was founded in 1966. The ongoing battles between the loyalist paramilitary groups and the nationalist paramilitary groups made up a big part of what the people of Northern Ireland call "The Troubles." This is the background against which Patrick's story unfolded.

Patrick was born and raised in Northern Ireland. His family was Catholic and they were nationalists, those who wanted independence from England. The IRA recruited him when he was a teenager. Bombing certain key targets had always been a part of the IRA's military strategy, so they trained Patrick in the art of blowing things up. He learned about explosives, fuses, and detonators. He learned about the difference between bombs intended to kill people and those intended to destroy buildings. For years, he participated in the IRA's war against England and the loyalists. Then something happened.

Patrick was eating lunch one afternoon in a pub frequented by members of the IRA. On this particular afternoon, one of the loyalist paramilitary groups had planted a bomb in the pub. Patrick was midbite when it went off. It blew him across the room and knocked him out. When he came to, the room was filled with smoke. Some people were moaning, others were screaming, and some were silent because they were dead.

Patrick smiled when he told the next part of the story. The bomb had deposited someone's roast beef sandwich all over his face and upper torso. When he regained consciousness, he was understandably groggy. In this muddled state, he thought the roast beef was his shredded body. Frantically, he began to search through all the "gore" to see where the damage was. It took a minute of feverish self-examination before he realized he was still pretty much intact. Such was the life of an IRA bomber.

God used incidents such as these to get Patrick's attention. He began to think more about his Catholic background. Before this, it had been little more than an institutional affiliation, just a part of what it meant to be in the IRA. That started to change. He began to see that Christianity was about Jesus Christ, and Patrick began a relationship with him.

As his relationship with Jesus began to grow, Patrick began to rethink what he was doing. He came to the conclusion he could better serve Northern Ireland by working for the healing of the country rather than attempting to identify and eliminate its enemies, whoever they were. He began to seek out like-minded people and found some within a growing group of people who called themselves the Cross Community. This community had a secular branch. They regarded the term *cross* as a reference to crossing the barriers between the factions in Belfast and Northern Ireland. But the Cross Community also had a faith-based branch consisting of committed Christians, both Catholics and Protestants. They felt that the best way to serve Jesus was to work for reconciliation. For them, the term *cross* had an added dimension—their work was anchored by the reconciling work that Jesus accomplished between God and humanity on the cross. It was with this latter group that Patrick made his deepest connection.

Both the secular and faith-based components of the Cross Community keenly felt the tragedy that had characterized life in Northern Ireland. Thousands of people had died over the years in the battle between the nationalists and the loyalists, and their British army counterparts. The Cross Community began to place itself in the middle of this bloody conflict by creating opportunities for nationalists and loyalists to sit down and talk, but the deep-seated animosity the two groups felt toward each other made this an extremely difficult process. So they tried to figure out things to do together that would contribute to the healing and health of the community. One of those efforts involved Habitat for Humanity.

THE PAST REDEEMED

As Patrick continued to involve himself in the Cross Community's work, he met Peter Farquharson, director of the newly formed Habitat for Humanity Belfast. Peter saw the value that Patrick could bring to

Habitat's plan to build affordable housing in certain parts of the city. The building skills Patrick had learned through his IRA involvement would benefit this effort. But more important was his status as an IRA member who had become a follower of Christ and had affiliated himself with the Cross Community. This would go a long way toward legitimizing the work of reconciliation that Habitat attempted to accomplish in neighborhoods such as the Lower Falls. Peter offered Patrick the job of construction supervisor, and Patrick accepted.

At the time, I was working at the American Church in London as an associate pastor. Our congregation consisted mainly of American expats—US citizens temporarily working overseas. At the time, there were upward of thirty thousand Americans working in and around London. One of my jobs at the American Church was to work with expat high school students. I had seen the way God used short-term mission trips in the lives of high school students back in the States, so I was eager to put one together for the expat kids in London. My boss, Jim Schmidt, suggested I check out Habitat for Humanity. That's how we connected with their work in Belfast.

But there's something you need to know about all of this. While we were planning this trip, the IRA was conducting a bombing campaign in central London. The IRA wasn't necessarily trying to kill people, just trying to make life miserable for them. The difference between these two agendas seemed rather insignificant to me. In any event, in order to minimize loss of life, the IRA would plant a bomb somewhere in London and then call the police to alert them about the general area where the bomb was and approximately when it was set to go off. IRA members had a code word they used so that the authorities knew it was legitimate and not a prank.

They never gave the police enough time to both evacuate people and find the bomb, so the police obviously focused on clearing the area first. As a result, about once a month there would be a section of London cordoned off while the authorities evacuated the area. Sometimes they would find and defuse the bomb despite the IRA's efforts; sometimes they wouldn't and the bomb would explode. Other times there was no bomb.

Given all of this, it seemed at first like utter insanity to propose taking a bunch of high school students to Belfast, the city from which most of the IRA activity originated. But the irony was that, as regards to the IRA's bombing campaign, it was safer at that point in time to be in Belfast than in London. I persuaded the kids' parents of that fact. So one spring morning, I—along with my father-in-law, Ken Sharp; some other adult sponsors; and a bunch of high school kids—boarded an Aer Lingus jet and flew from London to Belfast.

Staff members of Habitat Belfast met us at the airport and drove us to our first stop, a meeting room in the central part of town. There we met Peter Farquharson, who led us through what we would be doing for the next five days. After an orientation, we were loaded into vans for the drive to the construction site in the Lower Falls. After traveling for twenty minutes, we came to what was known as a "peace wall." These were fifteen-foot-high walls, often topped with barbed wire. They were intended to separate the nationalist parts of town from the loyalist parts of town in the hopes of preventing nationalists and loyalists from killing one another. Whether the walls did any good depends on whom you talk to.

In order to cross, we had to pass through a military checkpoint manned by British army troops. They wore body armor and carried automatic weapons. There was an armored personnel carrier parked off to the side. We were obviously in a war zone. This was before cell phones—I was glad the parents weren't going to see any of this.

The soldiers asked our driver several questions. Why on earth was he taking a bunch of American kids into the Lower Falls? Finally, persuaded that we were not terrorists and after sliding a mirror under the van to look for bombs, they let us through.

The scenery began to change. Murals began to appear, depicting people and events in the life of the nationalist community. Often the people depicted had died for the cause. Flags with green, white, and orange vertical stripes—the flag that had been adopted by the nationalists and represented their commitment to creating an independent Northern Ireland—appeared on the tops of buildings. We turned off the main street and then made another turn or two, finally pulling into a cul-de-sac.

As I hopped out of the van, a man in his early forties came up to me and smiled. He introduced himself as Patrick Donnelly and then said, "You're very welcome here, John." And he was right. In the IRA's backyard, in the middle of something like a war zone, all of a sudden I felt very welcome. If anyone could be a bridge between the nationalists and the loyalists, it was this man.

A MESSY MENTOR

We spent the next five days helping Patrick and his crew as they worked on the Habitat construction site. The high school kids fell in love with Patrick. None of us really knew what we were doing when it came to construction, but Patrick was unfailingly patient.

He would tease us about our ineptness. He would teach us how to do things. He would tell us the Irish names of the food we ate for lunch. My favorite was the name for the french fry sandwiches we would often eat. They called the sandwich a "chip butty."

We listened to Patrick's stories and the stories of his colleagues. We gained an appreciation for the depth of ill will that existed between the English and the working-class Irish nationalists. It made their resolve to seek reconciliation in the name of Jesus all the more remarkable. Their passion to see the Troubles of Belfast healed was palpable. We also met the people who lived in the neighborhood. We met their children. They were glad to see Americans and were pleased that we were trying to help.

After a few days, I noticed there were young men loitering around the area. They would lean against a lamppost or stroll past the construction site on their way to somewhere. When I asked Patrick about them, he said, "Those are just the lads keeping an eye on us." "The lads" were IRA foot soldiers. They had been assigned to monitor the situation and keep an eye on Patrick. I learned that leaving the IRA is not an easy thing to do. My admiration for Patrick grew by the day.

There were other organizations keeping an eye on us too. Several days in a row, a helicopter hovered maybe a half mile above the construction site. Again, I asked Patrick what was going on. "Oh," he said, "that's the RUC keeping an eye on us as well." RUC stands for the Royal Ulster Constabulary—the Belfast police force. The RUC was thought by many to be in collusion with loyalist paramilitaries. Others, however, thought the RUC was one of the most professional policing operations in the world. Apparently, the RUC surveillance included taking photos of Patrick and me. They didn't know Patrick had become a Christian. As far as they knew, he was still a suspected terrorist. And now, they had photos of me with him in the IRA's backyard. As a result, for the next several years, whenever I traveled internationally, it was not unusual for me to be pulled out of line at the airport and questioned by law enforcement officials. Clearly, I had made it onto a list that flagged me as having connections with a terrorist organization.

Over the years, I got to see Patrick a number of times. We went back to Belfast on another short-term trip the following year. Patrick and Peter Farquharson came to visit us in London once or twice. Several years later, after we had moved back to the States, Patrick and Peter came for a visit. They are two of the finest men I know.

I gradually lost touch with Patrick. I heard through Peter that the IRA made things difficult for Patrick. They knew where he lived. Among other things, they would sometimes park in front of Patrick's house and just stare at him and his family as they came and went. That menacing presence took its toll on Patrick. He knew what these men were capable of doing. He worried that someday they might do more than just look. Peter said that, had Patrick not done so much for the neighborhoods in the Lower Falls, the IRA's punishment for leaving might have been much worse.

When it's all said and done, the most remarkable thing about Patrick is that he stayed in Belfast. He could have left. Some would argue that he *should* have left. But Patrick felt that God had called him to stay. Few, if any, had the background he did, which gave credibility to his efforts to bring reconciliation between the warring factions. It had been a mess for decades. At one time Patrick was lost in this mess. But he had a strong sense that Jesus had rescued him from it so he could help the others still in it. It was a costly decision that Patrick always downplayed. We came to realize the situation was usually much more serious than Patrick let on. But that's the kind of thing you expect from people like Patrick. They would rather move toward the mess than talk about it.

As you reflect on Patrick's story, you'll notice that there's something missing. This is actually a good thing. We would all be healthier and more effective if this thing were missing from our lives as well. Perhaps you can guess what it is. But if not, no worries. We'll get to it in the next chapter.

If you would like to learn more about Habitat for Humanity Belfast, which is now Habitat for Humanity Northern Ireland, contact Jenny Williams at jennyw@habitatni.co.uk.

DISCUSSION QUESTIONS

1. Have you ever been involved on a work site with Habitat for Humanity or a similar organization? If so, where was it and what were you building?

2. How much did you know about the Troubles in Northern Ireland before reading this chapter? What strikes you most about these problems?

3. Even though the process is still ongoing, Christians in Northern Ireland have played a role in the work of reconciliation between

nationalists and loyalists. Have Christians ever played a similar role in the States? If so, what are the details?

4. Has your life ever been directly affected by a terrorist campaign? What were the circumstances surrounding that? How did it make you feel?

5. Have you ever met anyone like Patrick Donnelly? If so, under what circumstances did you meet?

6. Why is moving toward the mess sometimes so costly?

Chapter 7

THE GREAT IMPOSTOR

There's no problem so awful that you can't add
some guilt to it and make it even worse.
—Calvin, *Calvin and Hobbes*

A spiritual cancer is ravaging the church in America. It twists the Christian life into a caricature of what God intends it to be. It warps our understanding of our heavenly Father. It robs the cross of its power. It makes Christianity look unattractive to any marginally healthy unbeliever. And it turns moving toward the mess into a graceless tangle of joyless religious legalism. And you know what? I bet it's something you or somebody you know struggles with.

The spiritual cancer I'm talking about is chronic guilt. Of course there is such a thing as appropriate guilt—a periodic pang of guilt can discourage us from doing something destructive. But that's not what we're talking about here. We're talking about guilt that has become constant and malignant. We start feeling guilty all the time about all sorts of things. That kind of guilt can kill your faith.

For years I was completely upside down about guilt. The crazy thing is that while this was going on I could give you a detailed, theologically accurate account of Christ's atoning work on the cross. I sang songs about the love of God. I wrote songs about the love of God. I even went to seminary and wrote papers on salvation by grace. But when all was said and done, my spiritual life was largely driven by guilt. It was malignant and fooled me into thinking it was a holy motive. But it was not. It's the great impostor.

By malignant guilt, I mean guilt that provides an ongoing emotional background for our lives. My experience of malignant guilt turned on the distinct feeling that God's love for me was contingent on me doing things exactly right. If I didn't do things exactly right—whether it was having a quiet time or sharing my faith or whatever—then *wham!* The guilt moved from the background to the forefront of my mind. It became this angry, accusatory voice in my head that started shouting at me. For years I thought this angry voice was God's voice. For years I did things because I was afraid that if I didn't, God would take away something dear to me. I seldom worried about hell. I just worried about God punishing me in this life. I don't mean to suggest there were never times of peace and joy. There were. But these times were often bookended by fear and guilt. I've often wondered why this happened. I think it was a mixture of my wiring, my family system, and some bad teaching I was exposed to in the early days of my relationship with Jesus.

To begin with, I'm prone to worry, which I inherited from my mom. She was wonderful in many ways, but if there were ever an Olympic event for worrying, she would have taken home the gold medal. On top of that, I have an overactive conscience. I can obsess for days about a negative turn in a relationship, in an event, or in a conversation. When I became a Christian, I began to associate these dysfunctions with God. It took a lot of good theology and a lot of good conversation to begin to turn the tide, to realize that the angry voice in my head is not God's voice. By the way, I still hear the angry voice on occasion. If I ignore it or chase it away with a few key scriptures, it eventually goes away. Truth be told, sometimes it sneaks back and can make a compelling case for being the voice of God. Old habits die hard.

All of this was reinforced during my sophomore year in college, in the form of a seminar that toured throughout the country. It was characterized by a big red notebook given to all the participants. I suppose some good came out of it, but the main thing I took away from the seminar was a bone-crushing sense of guilt. "Do exactly what God says, exactly when he says it, or he will burn your life down to ash!" That probably wasn't in the notebook, but that's pretty much what I took away from the experience.

I hope that didn't happen to everyone who went to the seminar. Maybe it was exacerbated by my wiring and upbringing. But now that I think about it, while my upbringing may have made it worse, the content of the seminar was laced with plain ol' toxic legalism. So be careful what kind of teaching you place yourself and your family under. The fact that your kid is at some sort of school, camp, or retreat labeled "Christian" doesn't mean everything is hunky-dory. As the apostle John said, "Beloved, do not believe every spirit, but test the spirits to see whether they are of God; for many false prophets have gone out into the world" (1 John 4:1). If bad teaching were always obvious, there would be no need to test it.

Now don't get me wrong. There is a lot of wonderful teaching out there. But interspersed with the wonderful stuff is some very dangerous stuff. The toxic teaching I breathed in just about killed my faith. Thankfully, God's grace broke through just in the nick of time. So be vigilant. Think critically. Learn to weigh the teaching you hear against the texts of the Old and New Testaments. The faith you save may be your own.

GROUND DOWN BY GUILT

What's all of this got to do with moving toward the mess? Just this: doing the right thing for the wrong reasons is ultimately just as dysfunctional as doing the wrong thing. Granted, the realm of motives is the final frontier in our spiritual lives. There is a sense in which they will never be completely pure this side of heaven. But that doesn't mean we should ignore them. So fasten your seat belt. We're going to put guilt in its proper place. The problem is, it doesn't want to go there. And we'll also see that we often don't want it to.

We'll begin with a working assumption. Guilt is analogous to physical pain. Pain is that brilliant sensation produced by a nervous system that God has hardwired into the human body. When the system is working properly, it minimizes all sorts of physically destructive behavior. For example, if you're camping and accidently put your hand in the campfire, pain will motivate you to remove your hand from the flames rather quickly. Had there been no pain, you might have inadvertently left your hand in the fire long enough to render it permanently useless. In other words, pain is the body's alarm system. When a physically destructive behavior occurs, it sounds the alarm and says, "Stop that!" And we do—pretty darn quick.

But sometimes the system becomes dysfunctional. Something that's intended to be a brief alarm refuses to turn off. Then we're in trouble. Chronic pain means that something in our body has broken. When this happens, pain ceases to alert us to a problem. It becomes the problem. We can say the same thing about guilt. But often we don't.

The original idea, if I've read the owner's manual correctly, ascribes to guilt the same function that is attributed to pain. The difference is that guilt is a bit more preemptive in nature. It's the spiritual alarm system that says, "Don't do that!" And if everything is working correctly, we don't do whatever we were thinking of doing. A negative outcome is avoided.

Here's the problem: a disturbing percentage of us deal with chronic guilt. We would never accept chronic physical pain as normal. But for some reason we think chronic guilt is not only normal but is somehow the way religion is supposed to work. It ends up being the motivation for all sorts of supposedly spiritual activity. We end up thinking it is a godly motivation. And when moving toward the mess becomes motivated by guilt, things don't end up well. For example, you may be a solid middle-class person looking at third-world poverty. Or you may be an upper-class person looking at domestic poverty. Either way, you are one of the "haves" looking at the "have nots." It's a ripe situation for producing guilt. So off we go ... moving toward the mess because we feel guilty.

FALSE GUILT, FALSE MOTIVATION

There are two reasons why this is a bad idea. First of all, Jesus never used guilt to motivate people. As a result, people in the New Testament never followed Jesus out of a sense of guilt. You'll never find a verse that says, "And Peter looked upon the Lord and felt guilty and began to follow him." The people who followed Jesus were motivated by wonder and awe. They saw what this man said and did and were irresistibly drawn to him. Guilt had nothing to do with it.

Now it's true that, on occasion, they did something that made them feel guilty. You can bet that when Peter denied he even knew Jesus on the night of his betrayal, he was overcome by a wave of guilt and shame. It was temporary and produced a change in behavior. He came back to Jesus. But in the long run, guilt wasn't the reason Peter followed Jesus.

This brings us to the second reason why guilt is a bad long-term motivation. Simply put, guilt is not powerful enough to produce a sustainable, fruitful, satisfying involvement in what the kingdom of God is doing in the world. Let's say you live a comfortable middle-class lifestyle. There's nothing wrong with that. Then you see a TV program about homelessness. All of a sudden you start to feel guilty. Here you are in your nice house, driving your nice family around in your nice car while the people you saw on TV move their stuff around in a shopping cart. Guilt starts to nibble away at the corners of your soul. You start to think that if you were any kind of a decent person, you would be out there helping the homeless. You're not really curious about the homeless. You don't really care about the homeless. You don't want to get to know some homeless people. You just feel guilty. It's not about them—it's about you and your feelings. You feel guilty and you want it to stop.

Enter your church's "Serve the Homeless Day." This is the day especially designed for church people to get out there and make a difference. You think to yourself, *Okay, I'll just sign up for "Serve the*

Homeless Day" and *I'll stop feeling guilty.* So you sign up to make sandwiches at the local soup kitchen. The day comes. You make a few sandwiches—and *boom!*—you're done. Now you can get back to normal. The guilt is gone.

The problems with this approach are as obvious as they are numerous. First of all, because you were there to assuage your guilt, you made almost no meaningful contact with any homeless people. They were just a means to an end. They were merely objects you used to restore your emotional equilibrium. So other than a few obligatory handshakes, you kept your head down and made sandwiches.

Second, because guilt eradication was your main goal for serving the homeless, your experience wasn't particularly satisfying. You didn't have any aha-moments. You didn't learn anything about homelessness or your city or yourself. You didn't really find a way to enjoy the morning. You just made sandwiches. So, until you feel guilty again, there is no compelling reason to ever serve again.

What happened is you basically inoculated yourself against serving. You "injected" a diluted form of the real thing into your system. The diluted form gave you a diluted experience and because diluted experiences are so blah, you'll never come back. Guilt was a powerful enough motive to get you down to the soup kitchen, but it wasn't powerful enough to get you to engage deeply. You just showed up to perform a task. Perhaps the best way to sum this up is to say that "should" or "ought" are never very good motives for moving toward the mess. They may get you out on the street once or twice, but they won't produce a very satisfying experience. In fact, I'm starting to think that if our only motives for moving toward the mess are that we feel we *should* go or *ought* to go, maybe it would be better if we didn't go at all. I believe Jesus alluded to this when he said it is better to be cold than lukewarm.

Despite all of this, thousands of people mistake "should" or "ought" for genuine spiritual motives. But guess what? Jesus never did anything because he felt he should or ought to. He had a radically different motive. It's one you can copy. It's the real religious motive, not the fake one based on guilt.

You probably think I'm going to say something about trying to drum up some feelings of compassion. I'm not. Don't get me wrong. I hope that at some point all our hearts will break for all who break God's heart. But I don't think that's where most of us start. My suggestion is that we move toward the mess because we are commanded to do so. It's about obedience. Check out Matthew 25:37–40:

> Then the righteous will answer him, "Lord, when did we see thee hungry and feed thee, or thirsty and give thee drink? And when did we see thee a stranger and welcome thee, or naked and clothe thee? And when did we see thee sick or in prison and visit thee?" And the King will answer them, "Truly, I say to you, as you did it to one of the least of these my brethren, you did it to me."

It might be tempting to equate obedience with "should" or "ought," but they are miles apart. "Should" places you in the driver's seat and makes your sense of obligation the ultimate source of authority. Once you've met the requirement of what you feel you should do, you are released from any further commitment.

"Ought" turns your attention inward to what you feel about things. Once you've satisfied your sense of what you ought to do, you're done. Obedience, on the other hand, places the ultimate authority with God. We move toward the mess because he told us to do so, not because we feel we ought to. It's a simple matter of where the authority resides—in your own soul or in the imperatives of the kingdom.

Visualize an eighteen-year-old in a marine boot camp. Why does he get up at four-thirty in the morning to do physical training? Because he feels he ought to? Because he feels that if he's going to be a good marine, he should get in shape? Nope. It's because he is under the authority of someone else, in this case a loud, adamant drill sergeant. His sense of "oughtness" has nothing to do with it. His behavior is based entirely on the response to an authority external to him.

But God is nothing like that drill sergeant. He is infinitely more powerful. But for all his power, he has chosen to treat us gently. The prophet Isaiah characterizes the Messiah as someone of whom it is said, "A bruised reed he will not break, and a dimly burning wick he will not quench; he will faithfully bring forth justice" (Isa. 42:3). God's not going to stomp around and rant and rave to make us feel guilty. But he will clearly and insistently call us to join him as he pursues "the least of these." It has nothing to do with guilt. It has everything to do with love.

Speaking of love, the story in the next chapter makes absolutely no sense apart from the role love plays in the lives of Rehan and Amreen. Joyful and guilt-free, they are two of the bravest people I have ever met.

DISCUSSION QUESTIONS

1. What role has guilt played in your life?

2. Have you encountered legalistic teaching before? What effect did it have on you?

3. Do you agree with the author's comparison between guilt and physical pain? Why or why not?

4. Have you ever "inoculated" yourself by allowing a diluted experience to discourage you from the real thing?

5. What's the difference between obeying God and doing something because you feel you should or ought to?

6. As you reflect on this chapter, what areas of your life come to mind?

Chapter 8

STAYING IN PAKISTAN

They love all men, and are persecuted by all.
— Anonymous, *Letter to Diognetus* (Second century AD)

There are certain places in the world where it's dangerous to move toward the mess. Pakistan is one of those places. Officially called the Islamic Republic of Pakistan, it was carved out of the side of India in 1947 in order to provide a place for Indian Muslims to call home. The problems in the country revolve around which type of Muslim gets to control the homeland. As a result, there is an increasing wave of violence moving through the country. The Sunni majority, sometimes fueled by the fundamentalism of the Taliban, and the Shiite minority are thought by some to be in an ongoing civil war.[1] While moderate Muslims on both sides are calling for peace, the future remains uncertain. Only Iraq and Afghanistan have more terrorist-related deaths than Pakistan. And the trend is moving upward.[2]

The government, in an attempt to bring about order in the country, has begun to implement a form of punishment that has been on the books for a long time but, until recently, was seldom used. Today, those convicted by a judge of certain crimes may well be hanged.[3] But so far this has failed to stem the tide of terrorist-related deaths.

In the midst of this chaos, a tiny Christian minority exists. It represents only about 2.5 percent of the country.[4] It is risky to be a Christian in Pakistan. Nobody knows this better than Rehan and his wife, Amreen. These are real people, but these are not their real names. When I asked for permission to tell their story, they asked that their identities be kept secret.

Both Rehan and Amreen were born in Pakistan. Rehan's family was originally Sikh. His great-grandfather became a Christian in happier times and brought his family into a church community in Karachi. Rehan made a decision to follow Christ at a prayer meeting at this church thirty years ago. When asked to describe his conversion, Rehan smiles and says simply, "He called me."

Amreen's family, originally Hindu, also lived in Karachi. Like Rehan's family, they became Christians several generations ago. Amreen began her relationship with Jesus when she was in grade school, at a Christian youth camp for girls. She grew into a lovely young woman with a vital faith in Jesus Christ. Because the Christian community in Karachi was small, it was not difficult for Rehan and Amreen to meet. They fell in love and were married in 1991. They have two sons who chose to trust Christ when they were in grade school. While being a Christian family in Karachi was not easy back then, neither was it particularly dangerous. All of that has changed.

FAITH IN THE DANGER ZONE

I first met Rehan and Amreen at the Marriott Hotel in Karachi, Pakistan, which is an unforgettable city. With a current metro population of almost twenty-four million, it is the largest Muslim city in the world. I was there with my friend and colleague Durwood Snead, who had asked me to join him. Rehan and Amreen had invited him to speak at a pastors' conference held at the Marriott Hotel. There would be about two hundred people there from all over Sindh, the southernmost of the five provinces that make up Pakistan. Durwood and I were slated to speak, via an interpreter, about leadership. It wasn't a great time for us to be there.

The publication of several political cartoons by the Danish newspaper *Jyllands-Posten* in 2005 had set off a wave of violent protests by Muslims. These cartoons had portrayed the prophet Muhammad in a satirical manner, often showing bombs and rockets sticking out of his turban. As a result, Karachi was in an angry mood. We often felt the piercing gaze of disapproving Muslims as we walked down the street. Although we had nothing to do with the cartoons, we were Westerners and therefore guilty by association.

It is important to point out that the majority of Muslims in Pakistan, while offended by the cartoons (then and since then), have no agenda that would lead them to retaliate against Westerners. But there is a small minority who do have an agenda. They believe that the West is threatening the Islamic community. This meets the requirements in the Koran for waging a holy war, or *jihad*. Literally translated "struggle," *jihad* is a nuanced idea within the Koran, primarily focusing on the inner struggle of an individual to submit to Allah.[5] But when an external enemy threatens Islam, the Koran authorizes the use of force to defend the faith and the faithful.

The hostile Muslim minority has focused on the second sense of *jihad*, turning increasingly violent. Terrorism-related deaths increased 28 percent in Pakistan between 2012 and 2013.[6] This is the reality in which Rehan and Amreen have to work.

The pastors' conference I attended is representative of what Rehan and Amreen do. God has called them to serve the embattled leaders of the church in Pakistan. While their work primarily involves pastors, it also includes doctors, lawyers, and other professionals. Their mission is to equip, educate, empower, and encourage these brave people. Amreen is involved in the work, plus she has a vital ministry to Pakistani women. She encourages them and helps them to see themselves for the valuable human beings they are. This is particularly needed in a part of the world where women are often reduced to second-class human beings. By restoring women to their rightful place, it is Amreen's hope that they will be salt and light to their families and communities.

The conference Durwood and I attended was conceived, organized, and overseen by Rehan and Amreen. They found the venue, arranged for the food, lined up worship leaders, and coordinated lodging. They also obtained the interpreters who would translate what Durwood and I said into Urdu, the national language of Pakistan.

Given the cultural tension, the conference couldn't be held the way we would do it in the United States. The advertising had to be done by guarded word of mouth. There couldn't be any signs outside the venue, no special hotel deals for conference attendees, and certainly no media coverage. Conferees stayed in places dispersed throughout the city, often using public transportation. There were no buses contracted to cart them back and forth between their lodging place and the conference venue. They would walk into the conference hall discreetly, alone or in pairs so as not to attract attention. The whole thing had the feeling of being an underground event. It reminds me of stories I've read about the French Resistance during World War II. But it's happening today, in the twenty-first century.

PERILS AND PERSECUTION

I don't mind telling you that I felt like a poser, presuming to teach these dear people anything. Their faithfulness costs them a great deal. They face aggressive, focused persecution. They all know Christians who have died for their faith, and they know they could be next. Any "persecution" I face pales in comparison. I'm pretty sure I've lost some Twitter followers because I mentioned Jesus one too many times. And sometimes at parties people try to conceal their drinks once they find out I'm a pastor. Durwood and I should have been taking notes from the conferees. I think every one of them is going to be famous in heaven. Yet they came to listen to us. That was humbling.

After the conference, Rehan had an adventure ready for us, as if we hadn't already had one. He drove us up to Hyderabad, about three hours northeast of Karachi. Hyderabad is on the banks of the Indus River. It is a city of more than a million people. The plan was to stay in the Dolphin Hotel, so named because there are dolphins in the Indus River. We would then wait to receive a phone call. That would be the signal to pile into Rehan's car and travel into the desert outside Hyderabad. We would arrive at a village where some Pakistani Christians had been sharing the gospel. The leader of the village had chosen to become a Christian, and as a result, the whole village had decided to convert to Christianity. We were going to baptize a whole village of new believers. Incredible!

When we asked why all the mystery surrounding things, Rehan told us that if word about this baptism got out, the more aggressive Muslims in the area might attempt to stop it, especially if they discovered American Christians were involved. By making the event as spontaneous as possible, it would minimize that possibility. So we would be called as soon as everyone "happened" to gather in the central courtyard of the village. We would drive in, baptize everybody, and then drive away before anyone else knew what was happening.

I asked why they wanted American Christians to get involved. After all, Pakistani Christians had led these people to trust in Jesus. Shouldn't they be the ones to baptize the new Christians? Rehan said that by bringing us in, an important message would be sent to these new believers. They would know they were not alone in their Christian faith. They would realize they were a part of a worldwide community of Jesus followers who cared enough to send people to stand with them on this important day. It increased the risk for us to get involved, but it was worth it.

We arrived at the Dolphin Hotel around 9:00 a.m. and waited as the hours ticked by. Finally, the call came at about 11:30 a.m. We hopped in the car and made our way out into the desert. Forty-five minutes later we arrived. The village center consisted of a few whitewashed stucco buildings and one or two deeply rutted dirt roads. Rehan introduced us to the Pakistani Christians who had shared their faith and brought the village to Christ. They didn't speak English, so Rehan translated. We sat with them in what looked like someone's living room. They seemed glad to see us, but there was tension in the air.

After a few minutes we were led to a walled courtyard in the center of the village. It was about half the size of a tennis court. Over to the left, sitting under a canopy, were the villagers. The men sat on one side, the women on the other. The men were dressed in khaki-colored clothes, but the women wore brightly colored clothes of blues, reds, greens, and yellows. It was stunning.

Durwood and I were ushered up to the front of the crowd. We stood with Rehan and the other Pakistani Christians. We were honored with gifts. We told them how honored we were to be there. We prayed together and then moved over to the other side of the courtyard, where there was a cistern filled with water. The baptisms began.

After about twenty minutes of baptizing one villager after another, we heard something that sounded like a truck pull up alongside one of the courtyard walls. The walls were high enough to prevent us from seeing the truck or being seen by whoever was in the vehicle. All we heard was the engine running. Everyone froze. We were all thinking the same thing—our precautions had failed. The bad guys had found us.

Thirty seconds passed. It felt unbearable. Then the truck's gears ground, and we heard it pull away. Smiles of relief broke out across the crowd, and we joyously resumed the baptisms. We never learned who was in that truck.

Here's the thing. What was a onetime experience for Durwood and me is a way of life for Rehan and Amreen. They must constantly be on guard. They have received death threats over the phone in the middle of the night. Once they had to leave the country for a short time because whoever made the death threats started to follow them around town. Knowing all of this, you would expect Rehan and Amreen to have a haunted look about them. You would expect them to forget how to laugh and enjoy life. But they're nothing like that. They are charming people. They are bright and witty, talented and well spoken. They could easily move to the States and find jobs as pastors. They could run a nonprofit organization here and probably make it a fantastic success. They could enjoy the religious freedom the United States provides. But Rehan and Amreen have chosen to stay in Pakistan.

God will probably not call you to move toward the mess in the way he has called Rehan and Amreen. He probably won't ask you to quit your job. In fact, in some ways it's easier to move toward the mess when you're not a "professional Christian." When you're a lawyer or a teacher or a musician, you're part of a community outside of the church. You have easy and natural access to the people in that community. You're one of them rather than a pastor or a missionary attempting to approach the community from the outside. As such, you won't have to move far to connect with people when the mess asserts itself in their lives. You can be that calming presence as they struggle with whatever it is. You can pray for them, love them, and help them figure out what to do. What a great place to be for anyone who wants to work with Jesus, as he loves people right where they are!

It's all about being faithful right where God has put you. God put Rehan and Amreen in Pakistan. That doesn't mean they're better than you. They certainly don't think that. You shouldn't think that either. But do think about them. When I asked them how we could pray for them, they asked that we pray they would be encouraged and that they would be faithful. The kingdom of God is advancing through them. They'll go farther and faster with your prayers.

Rehan and Amreen would say they are ordinary people. I have my doubts about that, but even if they are, they are doing something extraordinary. If you were to ask them how they came to a place where such an amazing life was possible, they would talk about the subject of the next chapter. They would say there's no reason what happened to them can't happen to you. In fact, there are a lot of reasons why it can.

If you would like to inquire further about how to support Rehan and Amreen, send an email to the author at john.hambrick@buckheadchurch.org.

DISCUSSION QUESTIONS

1. When you think of Pakistan, what comes to mind? What kind of country do you envision?

2. Do you feel as if we Western Christians have a fair and balanced view of the Muslim world? Why or why not?

3. Do you know anyone who lives in a place where it's dangerous to be a Christian? What's his or her story?

4. Most Muslims consider the cartoons published in the Danish newspaper to be blasphemous. Does Christianity at times receive

the same treatment? What is a proper response to blasphemy in a twenty-first-century, pluralistic culture?

5. What do you admire most about Rehan and Amreen?

6. How can you embrace and live out those characteristics you most admire in Rehan and Amreen?

Chapter 9

CHANGE YOUR MIND, CHANGE YOUR WORLD

Taking a new step, uttering a new word is what they fear most.
—Fyodor Dostoevsky, *Crime and Punishment*

When I was a young Christian, I would occasionally come across some angry street preachers. They seemed to pop up here and there. Sometimes they showed up at the beach. Sometimes they found their way into the parking lots of sports stadiums. But when they could set up shop outside a concert venue, they got really loud and aggressive. I still remember them yelling at people. They carried handmade signs with the words *sin* and *hell* in extra-large red letters. I seldom remember anyone stopping to talk with them. You got the feeling these preachers were more into yelling than talking.

There was one word they seemed to use a lot—*repent*. They used it like a club to verbally beat people over the head. They made it sound like an ugly, harsh, offensive word. Many years later, I learned the true meaning of the word. Granted, those yelling preachers got it partially right ... but they mainly got it wrong.

The version they popularized was all about stopping things. And there was always a threat implied. It wasn't just "Stop that!" It was "Stop that *or else*." Stop smoking *or else*. Stop drinking *or else*. Stop sleeping around *or else*. The "or else" part consisted of some variation on the theme of going to hell. Apparently, hell was the place all of us onlookers, otherwise known as sinners, would go someday. But when the street preachers really got wound up, you got the feeling that if you didn't stop misbehaving, God was going to kill you off early in order to whisk you away to your punishment.

So when I first came across the word *repent* in the New Testament, I was somewhat leery. In Matthew 4:17, Jesus is quoted as saying, "Repent, for the kingdom of heaven is at hand." In my young mind, the association with the angry street preachers was unavoidable. Not only did they not corrupt the meaning of the word *repent*, but they also warped my understanding of the type of person Jesus was. It seemed that he was one of them and that he was usually angry with me. It took years of study, prayer, and conversation to break down the wall that prevented me from seeing God's grace. Slowly, I began to realize that God wasn't mad at me.

Sadly, the character of Jesus wasn't the only thing that was distorted. On top of that, the message caused me to conclude that the kingdom of God was about only things such as not smoking or not drinking. It seemed very small and angry and focused on negative thinking. The street preachers told me what the kingdom of God was *against*. But they never told me what the kingdom of God was *for*.

It's not that I disagreed with the moral positions these angry people espoused. I knew immorality was destructive. It's just that the tone seemed so graceless and wrathful. It made God seem arbitrary and picky. I was looking for a majestic, breathtaking way to view the world. All I got was a list of rules, each accompanied by a threat. I ended up obeying not because I was overwhelmed by his love, but because I didn't want to get punished by the angry old man they made God appear to be. Thank God he eventually cured me of that idea. But for a long time all my fears were represented by that word—*repent.*

OLD WORD, NEW CONTEXT

As the years have passed, I've discovered that a lot of people misunderstand what the word *repent* is all about. It remains one of the most misunderstood words in the New Testament. The good news is that, with just a little effort, we can recapture its original meaning. And then, watch out! It opens up a whole new vista, a whole new way of thinking. In fact, that's exactly what that word is about.

The English word *repent* comes from the Greek word *metanoeo.* The most accurate translation of that word is "change your mind." So when we plug this translation into Matthew 4:17, we can read it as, "Change your mind, because the kingdom of heaven is here." When it's read that way, the call assumes a different tone. Our focus moves from a specific behavior to a paradigm shift that will influence all our behaviors. We move from wrestling with a bad habit to a different way of thinking that will change all our habits. What appeared to be limited and small becomes a sweeping summons to reorient yourself.

As is so often the case with Scripture, this verse unleashes a torrent of questions. Christ says, "Repent! Change your minds!" But what are we supposed to change our minds about? How are we supposed to do that? If we can be completely honest, why bother? Is it really worth it? If you're feeling a little nervous about asking all of these questions, don't worry. God doesn't mind questions. In fact, I think he sort of likes them. It shows him we're thinking seriously about what he's said.

So, as we reflect on these questions, the first thing for us to consider is that Jesus offers us a new context. That context is the kingdom of heaven. Before Jesus arrived on the scene, it wasn't here, at least not in the same way. Then Jesus arrived, and now it is. It began to advance through his person, gathering momentum as he called others to join him.

Thinking differently is necessary because the reality in which we find ourselves has changed. Our old ways of thinking won't work so well anymore. We happened along, minding our own business, only to discover ourselves in the path of the kingdom of God. It has invaded the kingdom of this world and intends to take it over someday. So of course we have to think differently. There's a war going on. If the military metaphor doesn't resonate with you, let's look at things from a different perspective.

Suppose you find out you're getting a new boss at work. He's very different from the old boss, so everything's going to change. The staff meetings will be different. Maybe they used to be stuffy and boring, and now they will be engaging and enjoyable. The language the company uses to describe itself is going to change. It used to be stiff and artificial; the new boss is going to find words that light up the team and tell a new story. There will be a shuffling of the organizational chart. There will be some turnover. Some old faces that don't like the new direction of the company will slowly disappear. Some new faces will show up. And the changes will go on and on. Some will be easy. Some will be hard. But the new boss is going to take the office in an entirely new direction. So hang on to your hats.

A SIMPLE SOLUTION

Here's the point of both metaphors: our minds need to change because everything else is changing. The kingdom of God is going to turn everything upside down (see Acts 17:6). If we cling to our old ways of thinking, we will be sidelined. Not because God wants it that way. On the contrary, he wants us to join him. But that won't happen if we cling to our old ways of thinking. In extreme situations, being sidelined morphs into something worse. We might find we're not on the sidelines but that we're actually standing in opposition to what God is doing. It's happened to people much better than we are. We need to be careful.

So it turns out this business of changing our minds isn't a peripheral issue we can put off until later. It's something we need to get on right now. That's why Jesus started off his whole ministry with this imperative. It's how we begin, and without changing our minds, we really haven't started. Which brings us to the next question: How does one change his or her mind?

Jesus has the perfect next step for us. If we continue in Matthew 4, we get to verse 19 where Jesus just met Peter and Andrew. He told them to do something, and that something is the answer to our question. It's simple. It's an elegant solution. It will change our minds and, consequently, our world. He said, "Follow me." That's it. That's the answer to our question "What am I supposed to do?" He didn't provide a plan or a program or a principle. He provided a person. He offered himself. You want to know what to do now that the kingdom is here? Follow Jesus. You want to find out what the kingdom is doing in the twenty-first century? Follow Jesus. You want to find out what your role in that is going to be? Follow Jesus. Discovering what God is doing in the world and how that affects our lives will come to us while we are on the road with Jesus. It's there that we will find our minds are changing. As we will find over and over again, he offers himself as the means to do what he asks.

If it all depends on following Jesus, there's just this one little detail to iron out. Where is he going? Where is he taking us? He is at the forefront of the kingdom's advance in the world. But in what direction are we headed? Are we going to the front lines, or are we going to stay back where it's safer? Should we pack an overnight bag or just go ahead and sell the house? Once we start to follow him, are we ever coming back? Will things ever return to normal?

Sometimes we get answers about the future by looking into the past. As we're wrestling with all of these questions, it will be good to reflect again on what happened when Jesus led the disciples in the first century. He led them to encounters with lepers and crooked businessmen. He socialized with adulterers. He touched unclean people with a healing hand. He spent time with people no proper first-century Jew would be caught dead with. It was all so confusing for his disciples. It represented a wasp's nest of issues. In short, it was just plain old messy.

Andy Stanley, the pastor of North Point Community Church, agrees. In his book *Deep and Wide*, he says,

It's gloriously messy…. We don't feel compelled to sort everything or everyone out ahead of time. We are not going to spend countless hours creating policies for every eventuality. Instead we've chosen to wade in hip-deep and sort things out … one conversation, at a time.[1]

Now you know the answer to the question "Where is Jesus headed?" We no longer have to wonder. He is headed straight toward the mess. If we follow him, that's where he'll take us. It's what the kingdom of God is doing in the world right now. It's what Jesus wants to do through us. It's the key to making your life count for something, right here and right now. It all starts by changing your mind.

There are a thousand stories about people who have done this. One of the best, featured in the next chapter, is about a young Texas preacher who changed his thinking about youth ministry. It not only changed the church where he worked but ended up changing the course of student ministry across the country and eventually all over the world. If you decide to partner with the organization he started, whatever boredom you have will simply be crowded out of your life. You'll find yourself on quite an adventure.

DISCUSSION QUESTIONS

1. Have you ever seen street preachers on corners or at sports events? What were they like?

2. How does the definition of the word *repent* sit with you? Do you think most people realize it's more about changing your mind than stopping a specific behavior?

3. In what ways did you need to change your mind when you began following Christ? How do you need to change your mind right now?

4. Do you think many people feel God is mad at them? Why or why not?

5. Of all the things he could have said, why do you think Jesus started his public ministry talking about the kingdom of God?

6. If you're following Jesus, where do you think he's leading you these days?

Chapter 10

NO MORE BORED KIDS

It's a sin to bore a kid with the gospel.

—Jim Rayburn

Gainesville, Texas, the county seat of Cooke County, is a town with an interesting history. It's located seventy miles north of Dallas and seven miles south of the Oklahoma border. Back in the eighteen hundreds, the town was a "recreational stop" for the thirsty cowboys driving cattle along the famous Chisholm Trail, which stretched from San Antonio, Texas, to the railroad yards of Abilene, Kansas. When the great cattle drives of the nineteenth century began to lose momentum, the locals in Gainesville discovered that the soil around their town was perfect for growing cotton, and they grew huge fields of the stuff until the mid-1920s, when oil was discovered in Texas. The oil boom carried Gainesville through the Great Depression, allowing it to fare better than most towns during that lean period. And then there was the Gainesville Community Circus, a focal point of Gainesville community life from 1930 to 1958. One of the largest all-volunteer circuses in the country, it gave 359 performances in 57 different cities. It was in this small-town cultural soup of cattle, cotton, oil, and circuses that one of the most influential nonprofit organizations the world has ever seen was born.

With a population of nine thousand people, Gainesville had two Presbyterian churches in 1938, a small number compared with the number of Baptist churches, who would eventually claim twenty-eight local congregations. The reason there were two Presbyterian churches in town is that some of the folks at the First Presbyterian Church of Gainesville had started to worry. They felt their denomination was starting to become too liberal, so they started the Westminster Presbyterian Church in the early 1920s and affiliated with a more conservative Presbyterian denomination. First Presbyterian Church survived the split, and after the ruckus was over, the members started to think about how they could make an impact on their little city. They built a consensus around something very positive—they decided to hire an intern named Jim Rayburn.

Jim had earned a degree in mineralogy at Kansas State University and was likely headed toward a career in either the oil industry or teaching until God called him into the ministry. He began his studies at Dallas Theological Seminary in 1936, and two years later, First Presbyterian Gainesville hired him to focus on building up the church's youth ministry.

If you've ever been involved in a church youth group, then you know how these things typically work. Someone decides it's time for the church to "do something for the youth," and by "youth," they mean the children of the adults who attend the church. Usually, the minister or the minister's spouse is charged with running the youth group, but it often turns out that the minister or spouse doesn't know how to do youth ministry well. So things limp along. Perhaps First Presbyterian recognized this pattern and wanted more for their kids. The fact that they hired a seminary intern demonstrates an extraordinary commitment to providing some sort of attractive option for students.

Had things proceeded normally, Jim Rayburn would have been left alone to do his thing. However, normal was never a part of what Jim Rayburn did at First Presbyterian Church. And youth ministry in America was never the same.

A REVOLUTIONARY APPROACH

The story goes that the senior minister at First Pres came up with a new idea. Instead of focusing exclusively on the kids in their own church, he suggested Jim Rayburn broaden his outlook. He even went so far as to suggest that Jim consider the local high school as his youth group. This was absolutely revolutionary, and Jim was energized by this new approach. He knew he would have to come up with a whole new way of doing ministry, but the more he thought about it, the more excited he became.

What if, he thought, instead of asking high school kids to come to church, he went where high school kids were? What if, he thought, instead of trying to persuade kids to come in, he persuaded adult volunteers to go out? What if, he thought, instead of making church kids comfortable, he focused on making unchurched kids comfortable, kids who would probably make the church uncomfortable if they actually showed up? By traditional church standards, these were crazy ideas. But in the back of Jim's mind, they felt strangely familiar. He eventually realized they were familiar because that was the way Jesus did ministry.

So it began. He started to hang out at the local high school. It was scary. At first, the church people thought he was ignoring their kids by going after unchurched kids. It took them a while to get comfortable with what Jim was doing. At the same time, the unchurched high school kids wondered what on earth this seminary guy was doing at their school. But Jim hung in there. He began to learn the names of the kids who didn't go to church. He got to know their stories. He went to their games and plays and recitals and concerts. He was there when they laughed. He was there when they cried. And, boy, was it messy. There were kids who were beaten by their parents. There were teenage alcoholics. There was sexual promiscuity. There was violence, crime, and all manner of things that, sadly, the traditional church tended to avoid or greet with harsh judgment. But not Jim Rayburn. He didn't judge. He didn't condemn. He and his growing army of volunteers learned to practice the unconditional love that Jesus offered the poor, the immoral, the broken, and the lost. Jim Rayburn and his volunteers moved toward these kids.

They didn't have policies at first. They didn't have connections or authority or any resources to speak of except for their courage and passion. But they were there in the middle of a messy high school culture, and they didn't leave when things got complicated. And something amazing happened. They slowly began to earn the trust of these messed-up, high-octane high school kids who didn't go to church. It started to become clear that they didn't avoid church because they hated God; they avoided church because they didn't feel loved by church people. But they did feel loved by Jim Rayburn. And so their trust grew. They began to ask questions. They began to wonder why Jim cared about them. And, ever so slowly, it began to occur to them that Jim cared about them because God cared about them.

As more and more kids began to trust Jim and his volunteers, he felt it was time to begin some sort of weekly gathering. But he knew a church wouldn't be the right place. The kids still felt unwelcome there. Then he had a brilliant idea: he would have the meetings in the homes of the high school kids he was getting to know.

He began to work on a plan for what these meetings would look like. He decided they would sing a few songs at the beginning of each meeting. But they wouldn't be church hymns. They would be the popular songs kids were listening to. Then they would do a silly skit or two to get the kids laughing. And after everybody was laughing and having a good time, Jim would get up and say a few brief, simple things about Jesus Christ.

He decided to call these meetings "clubs." He began to invite the kids he had gotten to know. And because over and over again he had proved that he cared about them and loved them just as they were, they decided to come. They had a great time. They started to bring their friends, and they all listened carefully to what Jim had to say about Jesus.

What started in one house began to spread to another and another and another. What started in Gainesville began to spread to other Texas towns. By the early 1940s, hundreds of kids all over the state were coming to these clubs. Jim wondered what to call this new thing he was doing. He decided on a name—Young Life.

Today, almost eighty years later, Young Life is thriving. Headquartered in Colorado Springs, Colorado, it has a staff of more than four thousand who lead an army of almost sixty-four thousand volunteers.[1] These people are engaged in ministries all over the world and make an impact on 1.7 million kids annually.[2] Many consider the twenty-nine camps Young Life operates to be one of the best summer camp programs in existence. Every summer more than a hundred thousand kids visit one of these camps for a week. They are promised, "This will be the best week of your life." After the week is over, you won't find too many kids who disagree.

While Young Life has a proven methodology for reaching un-churched kids with the gospel and helping them grow in their faith, it's important to note that its foundation is built on contact work. One of Young Life's websites describes contact work this way:

> Because kids don't care how much you know until they know how much you care, Young Life leaders show they care by going where kids are, meeting them as they are, believing in who they can be. Within Young Life we call the persistent going out into the world of kids "contact work." But kids just call it friendship.[3]

Contact work. There is no better example of moving toward the mess than this foundational ministry strategy. Young Life's website continues:

Young Life doesn't start with a program. It starts with adults who are concerned enough about kids to go to them, on their turf and in their culture, building bridges of authentic friendship. These relationships don't happen overnight—they take time, patience, trust and consistency.

So Young Life leaders log many hours with kids—where they are, as they are. We listen to their stories and learn what's important to them because we genuinely care about their joys, triumphs, heart-aches and setbacks.

We believe in the power of presence. Kids' lives are dramatically influenced when caring adults come alongside them, sharing God's love with them. Because their Young Life leader believes in them, they begin to see that their lives have great worth, meaning and purpose.[4]

Contact work is Young Life's version of moving toward the mess. Young Life staff and volunteer leaders see everything—the good, the bad, and the ugly. They see it and they march right toward it. Substance abuse? They see everything from alcoholism to heroin addiction. Sometimes the parents are even buying. Alternate approaches to sexuality? Yes. Cell phones now make it possible for high school students to share the most intimate details of their sexual lives with whomever they want. Violence? Let me tell you a story.

A DIFFERENT KIND OF CONTACT WORK

The first big event that occurred during my tenure as the area director for Young Life of Ventura County, California, was called "The
5th Quarter." (Football and basketball games have four quarters,
and this event would be held afterward, thus the name "The 5th
Quarter.") This inaugural event was scheduled to happen right after
one of the biggest high school basketball games of the season. We
made arrangements to hold it at one of those burger places that have
acres of tables.

We had started doing contact work at the two high schools in
town. We figured this event would enable us to do several weeks'
worth of contact work in one evening by bringing together a bunch
of kids in one spot. Young Life was still new in town, and we didn't
really know how many people to expect. We had advertised exten-
sively. We were hoping and praying for a hundred kids to show up.
You can imagine our wonder when a hundred kids showed up in
the *first five minutes* of the event. The line of kids—five hundred of
them—waiting to get in stretched way out into the parking lot. We
were ecstatic and a little nervous.

We discovered that two gangs had shown up. The first one was
called the Pierpont Rats. Pierpont was a neighborhood in the center
of town, right on the beach. They all wore plaid flannel shirts and
Seattle Mariners baseball hats. The other gang in attendance was a
Latino gang from Saticoy, another neighborhood on the south side
of town. We were thrilled they were there. They were just the kind
of messy kids we wanted to get to know. But while we thought the

gangs were there to participate in our event, it turned out they were there for a different kind of event. Their event was to take place in the parking lot.

I knew something was going on when the Pierpont Rats all filed out the back door of the burger joint. Because there were so many kids in the room, I couldn't get to them before they disappeared out into the parking lot. In fact, I could just barely move because of the crowd. Eventually I got out the front door and ran around to the back. But I was too late. Their "event" was already over. The Pierpont Rats were gone. A Latino kid was on the ground with a bleeding head wound. Someone said he'd been hit with a tire iron. Four or five fellow gang members surrounded him. When I tried to approach him to see if I could help, they "encouraged" me to stay away. This was before cell phones were around, so I couldn't call anybody without going back inside. As I was pondering my next move, a beautiful black '68 El Camino pulled up. The members opened the door, tossed their wounded colleague into the backseat, and sped off.

I stood there for a moment, trying to get my head around what had just happened. The party was raging inside. Our leaders were meeting new kids left and right. There was laughter and music and a huge amount of positive energy. I realized, standing there in the parking lot by myself, that if we were getting it right, this is the way it would be. That's why the mess is so chaotic. Good and bad, fun stuff and horrible stuff are going on simultaneously. There's positive, almost innocent teenage energy tinged around the edges with a dark, violent stain. That's right where Young Life needs to be—in the middle of high school messes.

Young Life is classified as a "parachurch" organization, meaning a Christian nonprofit that functions alongside the church, supplementing what churches are doing in the world. Well, Young Life may be "parachurch," but it isn't "parakingdom." It's the kingdom of God itself, disguised as a bunch of brave adults hanging out with kids the church either can't or won't reach. It's the community of those who heard Jesus's call to think differently. They've followed him out into the world. It's the restless and committed few who want to be on the front lines in this epic battle between good and evil as it plays out in the lives of unchurched high school kids.

Bored? You won't find many bored people among the staff and volunteers of Young Life. If this is something you would like to investigate further, go to www.younglife.org. Surf around. Check out the pages on "Mission and Vision" and "Philosophies and Methods." If you feel a tug and want to explore further, go to the "Get Involved" page on the site. There are several options there for you to consider.

One more thing. Take the time to look at the pictures of the high school students scattered throughout the site. You'll notice that most of them include an adult close by. Pray about it. Maybe someday you'll be in one of those pictures. It's an option to consider as you think about God's call to move toward the mess.

Next up, in part two of this book, we're going to switch gears a bit and start focusing on some actionable ways to put moving toward the mess into practice. We've also thrown in a couple of stories about the CEOs of two important nonprofit organizations just to give you more examples to think about. So put that coffee down and put both hands on the steering wheel. We're about to shift into high gear.

DISCUSSION QUESTIONS

1. Are you surprised at where and when Young Life started? Why or why not?

2. How do you think the members of the church received the news that Jim Rayburn's boss suggested he focus on the local high school instead of the "church kids"?

3. What do you think the kids at the local high school thought when Jim Rayburn started hanging out on campus?

4. Why was it important for Young Life clubs to meet in kids' houses rather than at the church?

5. How would you describe the concept of "contact work"? How does it reflect the idea of moving toward the mess?

6. What sort of person would make an effective Young Life volunteer? Is that something you would ever consider? Why or why not?

Part II

TWO CEOS AND SOME PRACTICAL ADVICE

Chapter 11

BOB CRESON AND WYCLIFFE BIBLE TRANSLATORS

If it gets harder to stay than to go, that could be one indication
that God is stirring your hearts and asking you to make a move.
—*The Finish Line: Stories of Hope through Bible Translation*

Fasten your seat belts. This is a big story. It started over six hundred years ago in medieval England. Today, it's playing out across the entire world. It began at an excruciatingly slow pace—one man translating one word at a time from one single language into another single language. But it's been picking up speed over the centuries. Now, it's hurtling forward at a pace unimaginable only a few years ago. Thousands of people are translating thousands of words into thousands of languages, 24/7.

You've never seen anything like it. And it's all rocketing toward a specific destination. Some say we'll get there within our lifetime. When we do, every culture on every continent will be changed. It may not make the headlines of your local newspaper. But in some places it will be the reason why the people there can read a newspaper at all. I'm referring to the work of Wycliffe Bible

Translators. Their goal is to make sure that all unreached people groups will have a Bible translation program in progress by the year 2025.

The numbers surrounding this task are daunting. There are around seven thousand spoken languages in the world. Dallas Creson, wife of Wycliffe President and CEO Bob Creson, points out that the organization recently catalogued almost four hundred different sign languages spanning the globe. Wycliffe intends to translate the Bible into every one.

Think about it. This means there are about seven thousand words and four hundred signs in the world for the word *water*, and another seven thousand words and four hundred signs for the words *heaven*, *teach*, and *go*. With that in mind, consider the fact that there are 8,674 different Hebrew words in the Old Testament and 5,624 different Greek words in the New Testament (along with a small number of Aramaic words found in both, which I won't include for simplicity's sake).[1] Together, that adds up to 14,298 different words in the Bible. Keep in mind that many of these words are repeated multiple times. For example, the word *Jesus* is repeated about 980 times in the New Testament, depending on which version you use.[2] Altogether, we end up with a whopping 783,137 words in the Bible.

If you open up the calculator app on your smartphone and multiply the number of different words in the Bible (14,298) by the number of languages in the world (7,400, more or less), you get 105,805,200 different words Wycliffe has to figure out, work with, and place into the hands of people who are hungry to hear what those words mean. I'm not sure the phrase "move toward the *mess*" is appropriate here—how about "move toward the most incredibly complex linguistic puzzle in the history of the world"?

Whatever we call it, this is the task that Wycliffe faces … every day. Bob Creson is one of those who think it will be complete within a generation. We'll hear what Bob has to say about that shortly. In the meantime, there's a remarkable story to tell about this remarkable organization.

BRINGING SCRIPTURE TO THE MASSES

December 28, 1384. John Wycliffe, a Roman Catholic priest, was saying the Mass in a Catholic parish church in England. As the service continued, it appeared something was wrong—John Wycliffe was having a stroke. Whether he completed the service is unknown. What is known is that he died several days later and was buried in a place considered to be holy, befitting a scholarly priest of his stature. But thirty years later, in 1415, church authorities dug up his bones and reburied them in a common unholy grave.[3] Then thirteen years after that, in 1428, they dug up his bones again, burned them, and threw the ashes in a stream.[4] They condemned his teaching and made reading his work a crime. What on earth had John Wycliffe done?

By twenty-first-century standards, Wycliffe's work would have made it into only a couple of articles in a Christian magazine. He might have earned a minor article in the religious section of *Time* or *USA Today*. But by fifteenth-century standards, Wycliffe was a source of constant front-page news. He basically did three things.

First, his theology questioned some of the foundational teachings held by the Roman Catholic Church, including their views on the Mass, the authority of the pope, and the process of confirmation. While this kind of questioning is routine today, it was absolutely scandalous, shocking, and dangerous back then. There was no separation of church and state in fifteenth-century England. The clergy had political power. They could have you executed for such things.

Second, John Wycliffe challenged the power of the clergy and the moral corruption that their power protected. He lobbied for a distribution of the church's pastoral duties among a much broader cross section of people. If theological confrontation was dangerous in the fifteenth century, questioning the power base of the clergy was suicidal. You were made to feel that you were rebelling against God and subject to all the hellish punishments God reserved for people who challenge his authority. In reality, all John Wycliffe challenged was a corrupt system that furnished the clergy with power and prestige. Even casual students of history know that too often, when people challenge the powerful, the powerful come after them. Because of an unusual set of circumstances, this response to John Wycliffe was delayed until after his death.

Finally, and perhaps most important, John Wycliffe translated the Bible into English from the Latin Vulgate. His critics accused him of turning "the jewel of the clergy" into "the toy of the laity."[5] He was passionate, however, about the common man having access to the Scriptures in his or her native tongue. One of the things that supported the corrupt power base of the clergy was their exclusive access to Scripture. Wycliffe's work began to erase that exclusivity. It gave the common man a Bible he could read and understand.

This was an act of revolution. No wonder the corrupt clergy moved against it.

Through these efforts, and many more like them, John Wycliffe laid the foundation for the English Reformation that would happen a hundred years later. His life pointed toward the power of Scripture to call out evil, disrupt it, and begin a process of redemption. It just happened that this particular mess was inside the church rather than on the outside.

Fast-forward about five hundred years to 1917. A then-unknown American missionary, Cameron Townsend, was traveling through portions of Central America, sharing the gospel and distributing Spanish Bibles. He was accompanied by Francisco Diaz, a young member of the Cakchiquel people, a subgroup of the Mayan Indians who lived in the midwestern highlands of Guatemala. At some point in their journey, Francisco pushed back a little and asked why on earth they were distributing Scriptures written in Spanish. It was not the native tongue of any of the people they were trying to reach.[6]

Cameron took what Francisco said very seriously. It became clear to him that it was crucial for every people group to have Scripture available to them in their mother tongues—in the languages that speak to their hearts. Not too many years later, Wycliffe Bible Translators was born. It took up where John Wycliffe left off hundreds of years earlier.

Today, Wycliffe USA is headquartered in Orlando, Florida. It is one of 130 Wycliffe organizations worldwide. The American office is home to about 300 staff members, not to mention the additional 3,600 staff members working around the world.[7] And it's not just an office building. It's a destination.

If you ever decide to go to Orlando (apparently there's some sort of theme park there), you should set aside a morning to hop over to the Wycliffe offices. You'll feel as though you're back at the theme park. There are all sorts of colorful multimedia experiences. There are displays with life-sized figures that represent some of the people groups with which Wycliffe has worked. They may not be audio-animatronic, but along with the sound track linked to them, you'll have a vivid, enjoyable experience. You'll also notice the crowd of people with whom you're moving through the exhibits. These people will likely be from all over the world. They may well represent one of the people groups referenced in the displays. And if you're lucky, you might bump into Bob and Dallas Creson.

As president and CEO of Wycliffe USA, Bob has the organizational title, but you quickly realize that Dallas is a key part of things. A moment ago, we fast-forwarded from John Wycliffe to Cameron Townsend. Now we need to rewind from present day to the early 1980s. There we find Bob and Dallas at home in Ventura, California.

Ventura is a small city on the California coast, about an hour north of downtown Los Angeles. It's an oil town, but today the economy is mostly based on agriculture. In Ventura, you're never too far away from lemon or avocado trees. They thrive in the cool coastal climate of Southern California, where it seldom gets over 80 degrees or under 40 degrees Fahrenheit. Bob and Dallas grew up there. They met at Buena High School, fell in love, got married, and attended Pepperdine University, just down the coast in Malibu.

After graduation, they moved back to Ventura, where Bob joined the family business run by his father. They built pipeline for agricultural irrigation and drainage. Bob's dad was a World War II marine who had participated in the invasion of Okinawa, one of the pivotal battles of the war. With the family business booming, those were good years. Bob and Dallas had four kids, attended a great church, and were part of a wonderful small group. How could it get any better? I'll let Bob recount what happened next.

> We experienced seven years of plenty—business was good. Then, all at once, there was a downturn in the economy and business dried up—a year of drought. Dad and I went from the best financial year we'd ever had to the worst.
>
> During the period of plenty, Dad had "retired" and was spending a good deal of time out of the office. Almost overnight our income fell to the point that I had to lay off most of our employees and ask Dad to come back to work. He and I both had to do things we hadn't done in a while....
>
> During that year of drought in the business, God dealt intensely with me, and with Dallas as well, about a change He would bring about; we just didn't know what He was preparing us for at the time.
>
> While we wondered what God was doing, He continued to provide for us (à la Jeremiah 17), but He also used the time to pry us out of our complacency. Having grown comfortable with our middle-class lifestyle, we began to examine how

we would invest the next portion of our lives. The more we thought about it, the more uncomfortable we became. As Dallas puts it, "We began to feel as if we had our shoes on the wrong feet!"[8]

It's worth taking a moment to investigate the uncomfortable feelings Bob and Dallas experienced. These feelings were the result of a divinely inspired restlessness. Even when the family business picked back up, they found themselves asking, "Is this all there is?" Or as Dallas put it, "There's gotta be more to the kingdom than this."[9] They felt somewhat insulated by the comfortable Christian community in which they lived. There seemed to be a wall between them and the rest of the world. It was subtle. There were no sensational events to which they could point as evidence. It certainly wasn't anybody's fault. Their church and small group were filled with enjoyable, godly people. But Bob and Dallas felt their vision being directed beyond the boundaries of their pleasant life.

At first they had to struggle with some things. There was the fear of losing the comfortable life God had given them. And what would Bob's dad say? Then there were the kids. What better place to raise them than in their hometown, surrounded by family and friends? What better way to nurture their faith in Jesus Christ than by remaining plugged into their wonderful church? And what better way to provide for their family than by growing the family business? If things continued, it would be a source of financial security for generations to come.

But the discomfort grew. At some point, it tipped the scales and began to outweigh the fears that held them in place. In fact, as Bob puts it, they began to become more afraid of the known than the unknown. The quote at the beginning of this chapter became their reality. It was becoming harder to stay than to go. It was 1983, and the wonderful town of Ventura could no longer hold them. God had other plans.

MAKING THE LEAP OF FAITH

Bob and Dallas began an active search. They didn't feel called to go to seminary or pursue pastoral ministry. They felt their gaze being directed farther afield. They discovered an organization called Intercristo.[10] Among other things, this organization administered an extensive questionnaire for people inquiring about overseas service. On the basis of the results, it would make several suggestions about possible matches with organizations and opportunities. It was exactly what Bob and Dallas needed. They filled out Intercristo's questionnaire and sent it in. The results came back with several possibilities for them to investigate, and the couple contacted all of the matches. The first organization to reply was Wycliffe Bible Translators.

They were instantly drawn to this opportunity. Because Scripture had always played an important role in their lives, it made all the sense in the world to join an organization that focused on making Scripture available to everyone in their mother tongue. They decided to move forward.

That summer they went to Norman, Oklahoma, to begin their training, and while there they were formally offered a place on the Wycliffe staff. Afterward, they returned to Ventura to raise support and prepare for their first assignment, which was going to be in Mexico, or so they thought. Through a remarkable series of events (which included a herniated disk for Bob), God redirected their plans. That's putting it mildly. The way forward went totally off script—that is, totally off *their* script. They ended up spending two years in Dallas, Texas, where Bob became the assistant to Wycliffe's vice president of development. In retrospect, God was preparing them for future responsibilities. But at the time, things looked fairly random. Since they still wanted to get overseas, they consulted with the organization's leadership. They were asked to entertain the idea of going to Cameroon. Dallas likes to say that their initial response was, "Great! Where is Cameroon?"

The path that led to Cameroon first took them to Paris, where they spent a year and a half learning to speak French. Fluency in French was necessary for the administrative work they would be doing in West Africa. In January of 1987, they boarded a plane for Yaoundé, the capital of Cameroon. This was to be their home for the next eight years as Bob took on the role of field director for the countries of Cameroon and Chad. It was a far cry from the comfortable life they had known in Ventura.

In June of 1994, the family moved back to the Texas office, where Bob became the international vice president of personnel. At the same time, Dallas became a director of personnel for both Wycliffe and its partners. Bob then transitioned into the role of international field director, where he oversaw about fifteen hundred translation projects. After about nine years, the next chapter of their adventure unfolded. Bob was asked to become the president and CEO of Wycliffe USA. So, in September of 2003, they moved to Orlando, Florida. It was there that I had the privilege of hearing their story in person.

CATCH THE VISION

You don't have to spend much time with Bob and Dallas before their vision for Wycliffe shines through. It is clear, compelling, and contagious. That vision is most succinctly set forth in a statement called "Vision 2025," which is to make sure that all unreached people groups will have a Bible translation program in progress by the year 2025. As mentioned, Bob is confident this will happen during the lifetime of generation X, if not before the last baby boomers turn out the lights.

His reasons for this goal are persuasive. The number of languages that still need a Bible translation has dropped below two thousand.[11] Simultaneously, there are about 2,100 translations in progress. These translations are no longer being done exclusively by people from the United States, Canada, England, Europe, and Australia—increasingly, teams from churches in Latin America, Africa, Asia, and the Pacific are doing the translation work too. These international teams have the advantage of being fairly close, linguistically and culturally, to the people they seek to serve. The other thing about these teams is that they are not limited to Wycliffe staff members. As the work of translation continues, Wycliffe has created partnerships with several different agencies. These organizations work together with them to translate Scripture into all the world's languages. These partnerships are crucial to successfully completing the task before them.

Then there are the software geeks. Translation is no longer done with pencil and paper, but on laptops uplinked by satellite to a network that updates linguistic databases instantaneously. And the software programs that make all of this happen have cut the average time it takes to translate the New Testament into a new language from twenty years to ten years.

The other thing about Bob and Dallas's vision is its breadth. It is as deep as the New Testament and as wide as God's love. Bob puts it this way:

> Bible translation has never been done in a vacuum, and the results have never been measured purely in spiritual terms. It's always been part of a larger package; it's always included ministry to a community's physical, social, and economic needs. And that ministry, now called holistic ministry, is an increasingly important part of the story.[12]

We could go on. Spending time with Bob and Dallas gives you a lot to think about. But here's the thing: The Cresons are intelligent and fun. They are well spoken and savvy. They like to enjoy themselves. They think God is the giver of every good and perfect gift. They don't come across as "superspiritual." They come across as perfectly normal. In other words, in many ways they are a lot like you.

But when you talk to them, you realize that not only do they have their fingers on the pulse of American culture, but they are also aware of global issues and trends in a way few people are. They got that way because, back in the 1980s, God asked them if they would like to participate in what he is doing in the world. They said yes and their lives started to fill with opportunities, challenges, amazing experiences, and meaning. Bored? They don't even remember what that word means.

God is asking you the same question. Do you want to participate in what God is doing in the world? He probably won't ask you to move to Africa, but he might ask you to walk across the street. He might ask you to drive downtown. He might ask you to engage with some people who are different from you. Who knows? What you can count on is this: Wherever he asks you to go and whatever he asks you to do will involve getting your hands dirty. It will be messy. That's where God leads us. That's where God is working in the world.

If you've gotten this far in the book, then the odds are that you're listening carefully and trying to figure out what God wants you to do. It's time to consider some next steps, so the next few chapters contain some concrete, practical things to think about. If you're going to move toward the mess, there are a few things you should know.

If you would like to know more about Wycliffe Bible Translators, visit www.wycliffe.org.

DISCUSSION QUESTIONS

1. If you had to guess the number of languages in the world before reading this chapter, what number would you have guessed?

2. In the section on John Wycliffe, the author points out that the clergy of the fifteenth century were angry that the Bible was translated into English. Why?

3. Do you think the Bible is thought of as a revolutionary book today? Why or why not?

4. How similar is your life to the life Bob and Dallas Creson lived in Ventura, California?

5. Was the decision Bob and Dallas made to leave Ventura based on guilt or vision? How can we minimize the influence of guilt and maximize the influence of vision in our lives?

6. If you were to take a small step (or another small step) outside your comfort zone, where do you think that might take you?

Chapter 12

WHERE TO START?

Start before you're ready.

—Steven Pressfield

I doubt you'll mess this up. But what if you do? You can just start over. The question of where to start moving toward the mess can appear more daunting than it needs to be. To begin with, the fact that you're asking the question "Where should I start?" is a good sign. It means that you are on your way to an experience that will greatly diminish the spiritual boredom in your life. You're going to be partnering with God as he works in the world. You're going to engage with people who will make you rethink everything. You'll feel as if you're in over your head. And you are. That sense of inadequacy will keep you dependent on God. That's a context where boredom is hard to find.

But no doubt you've noticed there are a lot of voices clamoring for your attention. According to the National Center for Charitable Statistics, more than 1.5 million nonprofit organizations are registered in the United States.[1] If you determined to investigate ten a day (which would be a lot), it would take you about 410 years to investigate them all. By that time, sixteen generations of your descendants will have come and gone. So perhaps we should work to refine the search.

Keep in mind that while serving with a nonprofit is an excellent way to move toward the mess, it's not the only way. It may not even be the main way. Remember, we're talking about a new way to live rather than participating in an occasional activity. We're talking about a new approach to life that will affect everything from your parenting to your politics. So this new approach to life might express itself by you volunteering at a homeless shelter like Atlanta Mission or by hanging out with your neighbor on Friday night. It might lead you to sign up for a mission trip with Habitat for Humanity in Ireland or to play softball in your city (rather than church) league. It might involve engaging with students through something like Young Life or reengaging with your own teenage children. The options are virtually limitless and the potential for making a difference is incredibly broad. In his masterpiece *A Christmas Carol*, Charles Dickens put it this way: "Any Christian spirit working kindly in its little sphere, whatever it may be, will find its mortal life too short for its vast means of usefulness."[2]

So the question isn't, "Where are the opportunities?" They're everywhere. The question is, "Which opportunity should you move toward?" And how do you decide which one God wants you to pick?

The good news is that there are some solid ways to figure out what God wants you to do. Some of them are a bit surprising. For instance, you'll recall the disciples had to pick a replacement for Judas, who had sold out Jesus for thirty pieces of silver (see Acts 1:15–26). They narrowed the field down to two men, Barsabbas and

Matthias. Then they prayed, asking God to show them which guy should take Judas's place among the apostles. So far, so good. But the next thing they did never seemed to make it into the books on discovering God's will for your life: they rolled dice. You might miss that because the text says they "cast lots." But I checked. Casting lots is pretty much the same thing as rolling dice. The idea, as I understand it, is that you ask God to cause the dice to come to rest in a manner that points toward the choice he wants you to make. It sounds a little sketchy at first, but then you realize it rests on some pretty solid thinking. So, if you want to use dice to figure things out, you're in good company. (By the way, Matthias won.)

I mention all of this to point out that God is quite capable of revealing his will to us in a variety of ways. We sometimes get a little OCD about it, feeling as though we need to say just the right prayer in just the right way and read just the right scriptures in just the right order. And of course if there's sin in your life, then the whole thing's off. Actually … no. If that were really true, then we would all be as clueless as a bag of hammers. While working on the dysfunction in our life is hugely important, if God waited for us to get all straightened out before he used us, nothing would ever get done.

STEPS FORWARD

The good news here is it's not that complicated. No need for all the stars to align at precisely the right moment. God's pretty good at getting you where he wants you, when he wants you there. For those of you who might prefer something other than the dice method, we can talk about the age-old principle called "follow the energy."

This is based on the idea that God sometimes directs us through our desires. It suggests that if he wants you to get involved with special-needs kids, he will get you excited about special-needs kids. If he wants you to serve people who are struggling with addictions, he will cause your energy levels to spike when that subject comes up. So as you survey all your options, where is the energy? What are you noticeably excited about? You should pay attention to that. It may be God nudging you in that direction.

My boss, Andy Stanley, introduced a slight variation on this theme. He asks the question, "What breaks your heart?" This idea suggests that the thing that really disturbs you, that really gets under your skin, is the area you should look at in terms of serving. So what really gets to you? Is it homelessness? Is it human trafficking? Is it child abuse? Does it have something to do with the environment? The issue that causes you pain that you can't forget about may well be the direction in which you should move.

The other way to focus your search is by assessing your skill set. If you're an accountant, you might be able to help a nonprofit with its financial systems. If you're a coach, you might be able to help coach a kid's soccer team somewhere. If you're a musician, you might be able to provide music lessons or concerts.

And by the way ... pray about all of this. Pray about the nudges. Pray about the energy. Pray about your broken heart and your skill set. And make sure you pray about all the other things we're going to discuss. Prayer is the glue that will hold all of these suggestions and ideas together and align them so that they're all working smoothly.

So let's say that, by using one of the above-mentioned methodologies, you create a short list of issues. These are all things around which you've discovered a good bit of energy in your heart. The next question to ask is, "Who's working in this area?" Of course, if you find your energy is pointing you toward befriending your neighbor, there probably won't be anyone. If you moved in that direction, it would be just you. But if you discovered some energy around homelessness or lack of drinkable water in certain parts of the world, then a little time with a search engine will provide you with a list of agencies, nonprofits, or task forces that focus on the issue that has drawn your attention. And of course the blogosphere, which contains opinions on everything, will have opinions on this as well.

Don't forget to check with your church. There may be someone on staff who focuses on missions and/or issues of social justice. The staff could be an invaluable help to you. If your church doesn't have anyone like that, surf the websites of some other churches in your area. You may well discover an expert who will be able to give you all kinds of help.

A LITTLE INVESTIGATION GOES A LONG WAY

The next step is to investigate these organizations. In 2009, Megan Springer, my colleague at Buckhead Church, and I led a team of people to Southpoint Church in Cape Town, South Africa. The church leaders were in the process of building a system that enabled their people to serve at some of the many local nonprofits in the area. They needed someone to help evaluate several of these nonprofits to see if they would be a good fit with what they wanted to do. What follows is some of what we learned on that trip.

To begin, we learned that just because an organization is focused on a worthy cause doesn't mean it's doing a good job. It doesn't even guarantee it's doing an ethical job. So doing some research is key. Again, your church or some other church may have access to data that can help you assess the performance of any given nonprofit. There are also some web-based organizations that specialize in evaluating nonprofits. Charity Navigator is an excellent example. This group looks at everything from the salary of the CEO to how well the groups document their board meetings. The National Council of Nonprofits, CharityWatch, and GuideStar are also options to check out in this regard. Different countries may have additional online resources to help with this process.

Once you have narrowed your list down to one or two vetted organizations, it's time to go visiting. Make an appointment. Ask for a tour. Meet the staff. If there are clients on-site, maybe you could talk to one of them, provided there are no issues of confidentiality. Be respectful and gracious. But pay attention. Do you like what you see? Do you feel that the staff are "on it"? Do they appear competent? Do they treat their clients with respect? Do the staff members work well together? Are things organized?

If you're interested in working with an international organization or an organization that's not in your area, then a visit might be difficult. You might be able to Skype with them or use Google+. Again, be gracious and respectful, but pay attention. And don't feel as if this is inappropriate. You are deciding how you and maybe your friends are going to be spending a significant amount of time and maybe even money. If things go well, you could be affiliated with this organization for years to come. So it's completely appropriate to learn as much as you can about them. If you bump into one that makes you feel bad about all of this, then your mission is accomplished. You don't want to get involved there.

KICK THE TIRES BEFORE COMMITTING

The last step is to take the organization for a "test drive." Sign up, preferably with a group of friends, to actually volunteer at the nonprofit you're considering. Make sure the organization knows that this is a onetime thing. A good one won't object, nor will the staff put on a full-court press to get you to make a long-term commitment.

Again, there are lots of things to consider. Was the experience well organized? Was there enough structure to provide clarity about what you were supposed to do and how you were supposed to do it? Were you supervised without being micromanaged? Did you have the tools you needed to do your job? Were they clear before you arrived about what you were supposed to wear and what you were supposed to bring? Did the task they asked you to do fit fairly well into the time allotted?

Here's the deal. Yes, there are a lot of questions. And yes, it's a lot of work to properly evaluate a nonprofit. But you're looking for a good experience. If you don't have one, even though you may feel passionately about the cause the nonprofit addresses, it will be difficult to hang in there. Moving toward the mess is an exciting and challenging way to live. But there's no need for a poorly run organization to make things more difficult. If you don't have a positive experience, you are under no obligation to return. We felt the weight of all of this as we evaluated and experienced some of the nonprofits in Cape Town. But it was worth the effort. Several years later, the church continues to move toward the mess by partnering with some of the nonprofits we investigated.

After all the evaluations and test drives are complete, it's time to make a decision. Pick one of your options and get started. Make a commitment that has a definite end date. Then you can evaluate things at that time and decide to make a change or make another commitment.

Keep in mind that it's never going to be a perfect fit. In fact, it's going to be messy. There will be easy times and hard times. There will be times when you feel passionate and times when you don't feel anything at all. There will be times when you feel you accomplished lots and times when you feel nothing got done. But if you've done a good job of vetting the nonprofit you're serving with, you'll see over the long haul that it's a solid partnership. And as for it being messy? Well, that's where God's heart is, out there in the mess.

DISCUSSION QUESTIONS

1. Has discovering God's will for your life typically been easy or hard for you? Why is that?

2. Which question resonates more deeply with you: "Where's the energy?" or "What breaks your heart?"

3. Where is the energy for you? What does break your heart?

4. How has prayer helped you in the past when you were trying to find direction on a particular issue?

5. When you think of moving toward the mess, are you more inclined to work with a nonprofit or do something more individually oriented? Why is that?

6. What's an example of a great nonprofit in your community?

Chapter 13

WORK TOGETHER

You cannot not minister if you are not in communion
with God and live in community.

—Henri Nouwen

In 1921, researchers at Stanford University began what was to be an eighty-year study. They wanted to know … what makes for a good life? What makes for a long life? What makes us happy? What makes us thrive and leads to success? They wanted the results to be driven by data rather than by a particular philosophy or worldview. So they began to follow the lives of more than fifteen hundred people. You can read about the results of this study in the book *The Longevity Project* by Howard S. Friedman and Leslie R. Martin. The book makes it clear that there are no guarantees or magic formulas. However, it does point out something very important: positive relationships are pivotal in leading a long and satisfying life. It underscores the value of making positive connections with the people around you. Here's how they phrased it:

Having a large social network, engaging in physical activities that naturally draw you in, giving back to your community, enjoying and thriving in your career, and nurturing a healthy marriage or close friendships can do more than add many years to your life. Together, they represent the living with purpose that comes from working hard, reaching out to others, and bouncing back from difficult times.

How fascinating to understand that those individuals who became involved with others in a consequential life would be improving their health as an unanticipated bonus.[1]

Pay particularly close attention to that last sentence, especially the part that says "who became involved with others in a consequential life." There could hardly be a more important insight for those who are seriously considering moving toward the mess.

MESSES ARE BETTER TOGETHER

Meet Brian and Jan Babiak. They live right outside Nashville, Tennessee. My wife and I have known the Babiaks for over twenty years, and they're the kind of friends who anchor our lives. They are important to our family. Our kids go to see them when they're up that way. If we were falling, we could call Brian and Jan. They would help pick us up. It just so happens that our friendship was forged, in part, on a construction project with Habitat for Humanity in Belfast, Northern Ireland. We also served together at the American Church in London, England. For us, they are an example of the reality behind the data in *The Longevity Project*. If I might be so bold, I want that kind of reality for you.

But relationships are time consuming and inconvenient. And so is this moving toward the mess thing. No one has a lot of time to spare. We are busy. It's so much easier for me to jump in my car by myself, zip down to the local soup kitchen, make some sandwiches for the homeless folks, and then head back to my life. There's no having to coordinate schedules with other people. I don't have to take the time to establish a consensus about things. There's no worry about hurting someone's feelings or making someone feel left out. It's so efficient when it's just me. I'm the rugged individualist, getting things done, like one of Clint Eastwood's cowboy characters. It's the American way, right?

Yes. There is a sense in which that's right. Working by yourself is efficient. It is simple. And it's also exactly the opposite of the way God designed things. It's when we explore why God designed things this way that we realize there's a certain poverty that sometimes accompanies efficiency. So the point is this: Do not move toward the mess alone. Take some friends with you. Here's why you should.

For starters, serving together is a richer experience than serving alone. It creates a bond between people that can last a lifetime. My relationship with Dr. Johannes Haar falls into this category. While I don't see him much these days, we are glued together by the fact that we were part of a team that served together for a week in the inner city with John Perkins, author of *Let Justice Roll Down*. Dr. Perkins had just moved into a neighborhood that, at the time, had the highest daytime crime rate in the country. His house was next to one of the busiest crack houses in the city. We helped clean out his backyard, which had served as a community dump, and get his house ready to serve the neighborhood. That was thirty years ago.

Then there's Shelly Stevens, who is now actually Mrs. Shelly Peters. She and I were part of a group that went down to the dump outside of Tijuana, Mexico. We served with a nonprofit organization that washed the hair of children with lice. There were, by the way, hundreds of little kids with this problem. When we pulled up to the small concrete block building where the washing took place, there was a line seventy-five yards long of kids and their moms, waiting for a shampoo. The experience was a shared memory Shelly and I will never forget. That was twenty-two years ago.

Dan Mancini and I were part of a team that spent a week in the Yucatan Peninsula helping a local church with its small-group ministry. Most mornings when we pulled up to the church, we saw a platoon of soldiers from the Mexican army stationed just down the street. It was a reminder of the struggle in which the community was engaged against the local drug cartel. The church's small groups strengthened the community, which stood against the evil and violence the cartel brought to the city. We had an unforgettable time. There are some hilarious stories as well. Ask Dan about the one involving my suitcase and the spiders. At least *he* thought that was hilarious. That week serving together is part of what defines my relationship with Dan. That was eight years ago.

There are tons of other people with whom I share memories of similar experiences. Brent Nissly, Dan Prout, Toby Nelson, Susan Fox, Katja Bryant ... the list goes on and on. The point is this: almost all the work I've done serving others has been done in the context of community. As a result, those communities will remain a part of me for the rest of my life. My relationships with Johannes, Shelly, Dan, and all the rest are richer because of these shared memories. We would have fewer stories to enjoy telling had we not done these things together. Our relationships would be a little less full. Was it more inconvenient to coordinate with them rather than just signing up for an experience by myself? I suppose. But the shared memories trump the inconvenience every time.

TWO DIRECTIONS OF TRANSFORMATION

Serving in community is transformational. It's not that serving by yourself isn't, but serving together leverages the degree of transformation in two directions. The first direction is about individual transformation. Proverbs 27:17 comes into play: "Iron sharpens iron." Serving together molds who I am. I am inspired by the courage, diligence, and grace of my friends. The friction that inevitably comes from working together provides opportunities for growth. We have an opportunity to move beyond self-centeredness. We learn to serve the team just as the team is learning to serve where it has been sent. As a result, I become just a little more of the person God intends for me to be.

The other direction in which the transformation moves is corporate, or collective. The community that shares a common experience of moving toward the mess, serving together, is transformed as well. It becomes less self-centered and more missional. It gains clarity about a crucial fact: Christian community is never an end in itself. It is always a vehicle through which the kingdom of God flows. But wait! There's even more.

When a group of people from the same church—or fraternity, sorority, neighborhood, team, or office—serves together, the impact on that organization is multiplied far beyond the impact one individual can have. Instead of one person coming back and telling stories of service and life-change, you have three or five or ten people telling those stories. As a result, more stories are told more times. The message is repeated more often. Ask any communications expert. Repetition increases the likelihood of changing behavior, even of changing culture. It works with one person, and it works even better with a bunch of people.

Let's get practical for a minute and talk about how to enlist and rally a team to serve together. First of all, you need to decide which group you want to mobilize. It's not enough to think about this in general. You have to get specific. Is it your small group at church? Is it a group of friends at your office? Your softball team? People from the neighborhood? Before we go any further, pray about choosing a specific group. You can obviously change your mind later. But the following suggestions will seem more concrete if you can think about them with an actual group in mind.

Once you've chosen a group, the first question is, "How do I get this group excited about moving toward the mess?" For starters, make sure *you* are excited. Passion is contagious, fueled by vision and stories and opportunity. If yours is flagging, don't beat yourself up. You can't guilt yourself into excitement. Instead, ask God for help. Ask him to bring people across your path who break your heart, who fire your imagination, who expand your sense of what's possible. I've found that God likes to answer those prayers clearly and often quickly.

Then start praying for your people. Ask God to do for them what he did for you. Be open. You may be the conduit to your group that God uses to bring people and stories and opportunities. Don't push too hard. Be winsome. Don't use guilt. Rather, drop the occasional enticing story into the conversation. Every once in a while send a provocative link their way. That and prayer can work wonders. I've seen it happen over and over again.

Once your group is excited about doing something together, it's time to choose a specific something to do. If one idea hasn't already captured the hearts of everybody, then bring three possibilities to the group and vote. Build a consensus. It's crucial that this opportunity excites people. So keep looking until you find something that lights everybody up! There are tons of opportunities—you need to find only one. It may be in your neighborhood. It may be in your community or a nearby city. It might be on the other side of the world. It might be with an organization, or it might be something you arrange on your own.

Not long ago, a group of people at Buckhead Church met regularly to take food to people living under the freeway overpasses in Atlanta. There was no nonprofit organization involved. It was not an official church function. It was simply an opportunity somebody saw and got excited about. This person became a visionary, a catalyst who mobilized a group of people. Human beings, created in God's image, were fed. The kingdom of God moved forward under the overpasses of Atlanta.

If generating ideas isn't something that comes naturally to you, a few resources will help. Consider these excellent books: *How to Be Rich* by Andy Stanley, *Love Does* by Bob Goff, *Crazy Love* by Francis

Chan, and *The Hole in Our Gospel* by Richard Stearns. Or go online and see if Habitat for Humanity has anything going on in your area. Be sure to check out the websites for World Vision and Samaritan's Purse as well. If you're still striking out, type "service projects" and the name of your town into your search engine. You will be pleased at the number of opportunities that surface.

After you have selected some options to consider, it's time to sit down with your group and make some choices. Keep in mind you're not making a long-term commitment to anything. You're just looking for an opportunity to try something out. The goal is for your group to have a positive experience serving somewhere. This could take a couple of tries. Make sure everybody knows you're just checking out some options. That tends to depressurize things. Then go ahead and make a choice. Sometimes it's hard to get the whole group on board. Peoples' schedules sometimes just don't mesh well. You may have to settle for not taking your entire group. As a rule of thumb, though, you'll want at least half your group to participate.

Once you have completed your first attempt to move toward the mess, set aside time to sit down with the group and process the experience. Some psychologists suggest that an experience always consists of two parts: the actual experience and the processing of the experience. Make sure you do both. Here are five questions you can use to assist your group as it processes its experience:

1. How did our experience compare with what you anticipated? Were there any surprises? Were there any disappointments?

2. What did you find most enjoyable about our experience? What was most challenging?

3. How did you see God at work through you? How did you see God at work in you?

4. When you reflect on what we did together, what person or activity stood out as something or someone you'll remember for a long time?

5. If you are willing to think of this as the first step rather than a onetime experience, what do you think might be the next step for our group in terms of serving together?

Before we move on, there is one type of group we should discuss specifically—your family. Getting your kids involved in moving toward the mess can be one of the most important things you do as a parent. It is huge for them to learn that following Jesus includes serving others. Their experiences in moving toward the mess will anchor their understanding of this biblical idea for the rest of their lives. A few parenting hours invested regularly now can be the catalyst in your kid's life for decades of service. Not a bad return on your investment!

That said, it takes a little extra effort to find kid-friendly service opportunities. Most nonprofits don't allow children under the age of twelve to serve within their organization. As a result, you'll have to look a little harder to find something for your family to do together. Your church may have found something you can do as a family, so be sure to ask your children's minister. If you need a little extra help, type "service projects for kids" into your search engine. Interview the organization before you go. You want to make sure your family has a great experience.

Here's something else to remember. Your family service group isn't limited to your spouse and kids. Think of brothers, sisters, cousins, and parents ... even elderly parents. My dad volunteered at a soup kitchen once a week from the age of seventy-six to eighty-four. It was the highlight of his day whenever he went. It gave him the opportunity to add value to the community in which he lived. Had I not been living on the other side of the country, I would have gone with him.

So here's the deal. What kind of memories do you want to share twenty years from now with your family and friends? Of course there will be all kinds. Some will be good, some not so much. But what if you went to Kenya together to help build a health clinic? What if you did a Bible study at the local prison? What if you staffed an overnight homeless shelter once a quarter? What if you befriended the cranky waitress at your local diner? What if, twenty years from now, you could look each other in the eye and say, "Wow, we were involved in what God was doing in the world back then." That's not a bad memory to have ... and to treasure.

It's time to hear a story about someone who has made it simple for thousands of people to work together in Atlanta, Georgia. His name is Jim Reese. His story, described in the next chapter, started in some messy circumstances. But those are the very things God used to get Jim right where he wanted him, as the CEO of Atlanta Mission.

DISCUSSION QUESTIONS

1. In general, are you the type of person who is drawn toward the efficiency of getting things done by yourself? Or do you prefer to involve others in your projects?

2. Do you have any memories of serving together with friends or family? If not, does that sound like something you would like to pursue? If so, which ones come to mind?

3. When it comes to getting a group to serve together, are you more of the point person or do you prefer to follow the lead of others?

4. What do you think about the concept of two-directional transformation? Have you had the experience of being individually changed and seeing a group changed simultaneously because of a project or outreach?

5. If you're reading these discussion questions by yourself, is there a group that comes to mind with whom you'd like to serve? What would be a first step in exploring that possibility?

6. If you're reading these discussion questions with a group, has your group served somewhere together already? How did it go? If not, is this something you would like to try? In either case, what might be the next step in exploring the possibility of serving together?

Chapter 14

JIM REESE AND ATLANTA MISSION

God has a bigger plan for men than just lining up for food.

—Jim Reese, in an interview with the author

Our culture places a premium on success, and there's a widely held consensus on how to get it. Start by getting good grades ... in kindergarten. As soon as possible, find a sport in which you excel. Get on a traveling team. In middle school, keep the A average and add in student government and some sort of musical or artistic involvement. In high school, keep the As coming. Continue all the extracurricular activity. Take as many AP (Advanced Placement) classes as you can and take prep courses on how to ace the SAT. Make sure somebody takes you on a college tour in your junior year. Pick several of the best universities you can afford and commence the application process. Hopefully, it all works and you get into the school of your choice.

You can goof around during your freshman year of college, but then it's time to buckle down, because your potential employers are going to ask about your college GPA. Do an internship somewhere and graduate with honors. Then go get a killer job. Make a lot of money. Get the right house and make sure it has a garage for the right car. Then marry the right person, have some kids, and launch them down the same runway.

There is nothing wrong with this plan—it just doesn't go far enough. It's not bad; it's just incomplete. There's more to life than our culture's definition of success. Ask anyone who has completed the drill. Yet this pursuit of success is normal and expected in our world. So when people step off this path, they stand out, especially when they've navigated the path so well.

Jim Reese, president and CEO of Atlanta Mission, is one of those standouts. We're going to look at Jim's story, along with the story of one of his staff members, Katie Patel. They, along with the rest of the amazing employees at Atlanta Mission, make it a stand-out place. It's one of those rare instances where a classy organization intersects with the messy world of homelessness. Jim, Katie, and the rest are quick to mention that it's not a perfect intersection. But it's pretty darn good.

UPWARD MOBILITY

Born to working-class parents in northern Michigan, Jim Reese had his world ripped apart in grade school by his parents' divorce. For eight months after the divorce, Jim's mom moved him and his two younger brothers into a new house every month. Jim now realizes they didn't have a home during this time—nothing resembling a permanent place to stay. Functionally, the family was homeless.

It was during this chaotic period that Jim became a Christian. At the same time, his life began to assume the trajectory that our culture associates with success. Eventually, he went to Western Michigan University and worked full-time to pay for it all. The people skills and work ethic he developed during these years served him well. After graduating in 1980, his career quickly accelerated. He moved through management positions with General Foods and Frito-Lay, each job more prestigious than the last. In time, he became CEO of Randstad North America, a publicly held company with revenues upward of $20 billion a year. By anyone's standards, Jim Reese had arrived.

Then there's another amazing person, Katie Patel. She is the marketing manager for Atlanta Mission. She grew up in Ohio. Her dad was in the air force and her mom was a schoolteacher. Katie grew up attending a Catholic church. When she graduated from Ohio University in 2007, she landed a great job with General Electric (GE) Capital. (You might have received one of your credit cards from this group.) The company moved Katie to the Atlanta area in 2008. They saw a lot of potential in her and encouraged her to get an MBA, which she did. Though it was still early in her career, things were looking very good. She hadn't yet "arrived," but it seemed to be only a matter of time.

So we have two people—a recognized corporate all-star and a young woman headed in that same direction. Our culture would look at them and say, "Way to go! That's how it works!" The thing is, it wasn't working for Jim or Katie. Jim resigned from Randstad in 2005, when he was at the top of his game. The problem was he didn't feel it was the right game for him. After a year or two of soul-searching, he accepted the president and CEO position at Atlanta Mission, beginning August 1, 2008.

A few years later, Katie met Jim when she started to volunteer at the mission. The more she volunteered, the more she sensed God leading her to do something different. She didn't want to wake up thirty years later and feel she had missed out. So, in 2013, she resigned from her fast-track position. When Jim discovered she had resigned from GE Capital, he hired her part-time to write grants. In November of that year, she moved to a full-time position as donor relations manager. In June 2014, she became the organization's marketing manager. And in the meantime, she married her husband, Akash, at one of the mission's properties on December 29, 2012.

The work Jim Reese and Katie Patel are doing is changing Atlanta Mission. As a result, little by little, the mission is changing Atlanta. That's what the kingdom of God does through its people and the organizations they build and run. And Atlanta Mission is built and run extraordinarily well.

To begin with, two of the mission's facilities, The Shepherd's Inn and Fuqua Hall, occupy a city block right across the street from some of Atlanta's premier tourist attractions. These include the Georgia Aquarium, the Coca-Cola museum, and the College Football Hall of Fame. If you know anything about homeless ministries, you'll know they are usually tucked far away from the wandering gaze of the city's tourists. Admittedly, the city of Atlanta had some concerns along those lines. But the fact that the mission was allowed to stay speaks in part to the quality of the facilities it runs. The buildings are clean and pleasant, always carefully maintained. The grounds look more like a well-run school than a homeless ministry. While that has obviously caused the mission to have favor with the city of Atlanta, it also speaks volumes about what the mission thinks of its clients.

If you spend time with Jim and Katie, you will quickly see that they respect homeless people. They understand that they are created in God's image and deserve to be treated as such. There is no judgment, no condemnation, and no condescension. Instead, there is vision. They believe that God has a plan for everyone. They believe that plan can lift people off the street and redeem their lives. They believe it can restore broken relationships and break the power of addiction. Given this approach, no wonder Atlanta Mission's buildings look so good. The clients deserve it.

This should not be confused with some sort of dewy-eyed approach to the harsh realities that face the homeless. Everyone at the mission realizes how hard it is to get off the street, to get clean, and to reenter the workforce. Everyone there can tell you stories about the people who didn't make it, who disappeared back into a destructive and ultimately unsustainable lifestyle. But the staff can also tell you about the hundreds of victories they've experienced over the years. Katie describes her job as giving her a front-row seat from which she can see what God is doing in the city.

WHERE TRANSFORMATION BEGINS

The mission statement for the organization is as straightforward as it is visionary. It reads: "Atlanta Mission transforms, through Christ, the lives of those facing homelessness."[1] Jim, Katie, and their colleagues have done a profoundly thorough job of thinking through exactly what transformation consists of and how it is accomplished. They realize that, ultimately, God is the only one who can transform people. But they've noticed that God seems to move more frequently and more deeply through those who have prayerfully given the process meticulous thought. As a result, they are moving toward a customized approach to their clients. They realize that one size never fits all and that homelessness is always the result of a complex mixture of personal wiring, family systems, and circumstances.

These convictions are leading them to develop a new assessment model for their clients. It will measure spiritual, emotional, physical, vocational, and social factors. They realize that a major problem in any one of these five areas can increase the likelihood of homelessness. They also understand that if these problems are not addressed properly, the chances of a client ending up back on the street increase dramatically. When the new systems are complete, it will be easy for clients to participate in the assessment process. As a result, each individual will receive personalized care using the best available methods and content.

Despite all the systems and programs that Atlanta Mission is deploying, Jim, Katie, and the other staff understand that, ultimately, God changes people through relationships. The assessments and services are necessary and very helpful. But by themselves, they don't transform lives. That takes people who are willing to spend time with the mission's clients. Jim calls these "life on life relationships." Without those, nothing much will happen. In order to make this happen, almost four thousand volunteers are trained and deployed by the mission. They do all sorts of things. They provide a wide variety of logistical and technical services. But they also give the clients of the mission a chance to form a relationship with someone who knows them and cares about them.

These relationships are woven throughout the five campuses the mission maintains. The Shepherd's Inn provides food, shelter, and a variety of short-term programs for men. Next door is Fuqua Hall, which provides transitional housing for men. My Sister's House provides a variety of programs and transitional housing for women and their children. The campus called the Potter's House has been around since the 1960s, but two new buildings were added in 2012. This facility provides a community center and transitional housing, also for men. And in 2013, the Atlanta Day Shelter for Women and Children merged with the Atlanta Mission. This facility addresses the needs of women and their children, providing clothing, food, hygiene supplies, and medical care. Altogether the mission's various facilities serve more than a thousand people each day. It is a shining example of an organization that has resolved to move toward the mess.

Perhaps one of the best ways to get a sense of what God is doing through Atlanta Mission is to hear the words of one of their clients. In their annual report for 2013, the mission tells the story of a man named Joe.

> In 1997, alcoholism caused Joe to turn his back on his career, his relationships and his responsibilities. He took up residence under a bridge on the east side of Atlanta, where he would live for the next 16 years. In the spring of 2013, a chain of events brought him to Atlanta Mission, where he has found the chance for a new life.[2]

In his own words, Joe continued the story:

> I was living under a bridge for 16 years. Now I
> sleep safely under the roof of Atlanta Mission. Me
> and God have had some very long conversations.
> He saved my life. I should not be here right now.
> Throughout my life He has been there. I came to the
> realization that He was walking with me while I was
> under the bridge. I feel Him. He has a plan for me
> or He wouldn't have me here ... I don't know the
> Bible real good, and have a hard time pronouncing
> some of the words. But I know He's there.[3]

No wonder Jim and Katie altered the trajectory of their career paths. Which brings us to one final thought. It's an important one: God is not against corporate America. Jim Reese and Katie Patel are not against corporate America. They can identify and celebrate godly men and women who move toward the mess by staying in their current jobs. And corporate America, by the way, is paying the salaries of the people who provide the financial support that keeps the mission going.

Moving toward the mess is not about leaving your job or staying at your job. It's about being able to articulate how your life is connected to what God is doing in the world. That can and does play out in a thousand different ways. It played out one way for Jim and Katie. It will quite likely play out differently for you. The important thing is that, somehow, it plays out.

In the next chapter we'll see a radically different approach to moving toward the mess. But it's the same kingdom moving toward the same mess for the same reason. God cares about people and is doing something about it. The crazy thing is … he's doing it through us.

If you would like to learn more about Atlanta Mission, go to www.atlantamission.org.

DISCUSSION QUESTIONS

1. Is the author's description of the typical path to success accurate? What would you change?

2. Do you know anyone who has left his or her job in corporate America to do something else? What's that person's story?

3. Why do you think the city of Atlanta was concerned about having a homeless shelter across the street from some of its major tourist attractions? How does this reflect our culture's attitude toward the homeless?

4. What sort of experience have you had personally with homeless people? How did that make you feel?

5. Why is it usually not necessary to leave your job to move toward the mess? When might it be necessary?

6. What opportunities are there in your city to serve the homeless? Is this something you or your group might consider doing?

Chapter 15

THE CHANGE AGENT

If there is no struggle, there is no progress.
—Frederick Douglass

What do you do if your church doesn't want to move toward the mess? What if you have a life-changing experience with a nonprofit organization such as Atlanta Mission and you come back filled with stories and nobody's interested? What if you went on a short-term mission trip with Wycliffe Bible Translators and can find nobody at your church who is interested in going on the next one? What if you've been volunteering with Young Life and are excited about seeing high school kids become Christians and your church's response is pretty flat? Most of us American Christians would solve that problem by leaving our church.

There's an old joke about a man shipwrecked for years on a desert island. Since he was a carpenter, he passed the time by building what looked like a little town. Finally, he was rescued. His rescuers were stunned at all the buildings the man had created. He offered to give them a tour. As they walked down the main street of the little town, they noticed he had built two churches side by side. They asked him which of these churches he attended. "The second one," he said. "So what's the story with that first church?" they asked. The man replied, "Oh, that's where I used to go."

Please don't be that guy. How is God going to change your church if you leave? Of course, he could change it in any number of ways. He can do whatever he wants. But if you observe the way he tends to work in the Bible, he usually changes his people through his people. So stick around for a minute. Let's think this through.

The first question to ask is this: Why is your church so uninterested in what you're experiencing? There are many possible reasons. Remember to be gracious. It may not be about apathy. It may be that your church is understaffed, overworked, and underfunded. It could be that it desperately needs people to volunteer for one of the church's programs rather than volunteer somewhere else. That's completely understandable. The church leaders are just trying to serve God the best way they know how.

On the other hand, the problem could be something I've bumped into occasionally. I call it the "Half Gospel Church." The gospel got divided up in America in the early twentieth century. Without going into all the details here, the end result was that we created two categories. The first is called "The Personal Gospel." That's all about evangelism. It's about leading people into a growing relationship with Jesus Christ. The second is called "The Social Gospel." That's all about issues of compassion and justice … things like homelessness and fresh drinking water in developing countries. So here's how this plays out.

A church that focuses on the Personal Gospel is going to be fairly uninterested in the Social Gospel. They see it as a distraction from the church's most important priority, which is evangelism. When the Social Gospel does come up, it's usually in a conversation about "those liberals." In contrast to that, a church that focuses on what we're calling the Social Gospel tends not to use that terminology. They just focus on issues of peace, freedom, compassion, and social justice. Evangelism never seems to come up. When it does, it's usually in a conversation about "those fundamentalists."

The vexing thing about all of this is that there is absolutely no partitioning of the gospel in the New Testament. I know. I've checked. If you don't believe me, then read it for yourself. You'll find there is no categorization of the Personal Gospel and the Social Gospel. There's only the gospel. And it's concerned about issues of personal salvation *and* social justice. Churches that focus only on personal salvation or only on social justice are working with only half the gospel. They are Half Gospel Churches. They are focusing only on half the mess in the world.

A CHANGE AGENT AT CHURCH

So what do you do if you find yourself in a Half Gospel Church? What if your church celebrates everything involving personal salvation but is tone deaf when it comes to racial inequality? What if your church rolls out the red carpet for people who champion women's rights but insists evangelists sit and be quiet? If that's your situation, it's important for you to realize that the church itself is a particular sort of mess. And like all the other messes, this is one toward which God wants someone to move.

Our problem here is that we have allowed the consumerism that defines twenty-first-century Western culture to also define our relationship to the local congregation. So we think of ourselves as shoppers. The various churches in town are different products. If we've been using "Product A" for a while and start to become dissatisfied, we start to look for a replacement. When we discover "Product B" (a church with a better preacher, better Sunday school, better youth group, or, in this case, a better approach to the gospel), we switch products, just as we do when we're looking for a new smartphone.

I'm not saying there is never a legitimate reason for leaving a church. But I'm suggesting that if you're facing a Half Gospel Church, you should consider changing *roles*. Consider a paradigm shift. Consider moving out of the role of consumer and into the role of change agent. You might be asking, "How is that even possible?" Good question. But what if this is the mess God is calling you toward? As you consider that possibility, there is an interesting text from Paul's letter to the church at Ephesus I'd like you to read:

> And his gifts were that some should be apostles, some prophets, some evangelists, some pastors and teachers, to equip the saints for the work of ministry, for building up the body of Christ, until we all attain to the unity of the faith and of the knowledge of the Son of God, to mature manhood, to the measure of the stature of the fulness of Christ. (Eph. 4:11–13)

Here are a couple of things to notice about this text. It's not the pastor-teacher's job to do the ministry of the church. It's the job of the saints. The pastor-teacher is supposed to equip the saints for ministry. That's a game changer right there. Most church people think their job is to show up Sunday morning and watch the "professional Christians" do their thing. Paul obviously had a much different idea. By the way, that word *saints* in this passage doesn't mean super-spiritual people. In this case, it just means Christians. All Christians.

Also, notice what this ministry consists of. Paul talks about the "unity of the faith." Unity is about taking things that got separated and putting them back together. This includes the gospel that was mysteriously split in half a century ago. Then Paul talks about the fullness of Christ. If we follow Jesus through the four gospels and define fullness on the basis of what we find there, we'll discover that fullness includes both our spiritual needs and our social needs, our need for salvation and our need for justice, our need for intimacy with God and the world's need for compassion.

We Christians—all of us—are mandated in this passage to make sure that our church's ministry accurately reflects Jesus and the work he did and continues to do. That reflection will displace the idea of two gospels with one gospel, one that speaks to every need of humanity. It's crucial our churches see that the mess isn't just spiritual. It isn't just physical. It's always both. The chaos, the mess, is at work in every area of life. Our church's agenda must reflect that.

So you've got your permission, your platform, and your marching orders, all courtesy of the apostle Paul. He wants us to move toward the mess ... all of it. He expects us to help our churches do the same. I've made some mistakes in this area, and I've got things right a time or two. Here are a few practical things for you to consider in your role as change agent.

First of all, you are not going to argue people into changing. You may be smart, well spoken, and able to think on your feet. You may have found several biblical texts that make your point crystal clear. Most important of all, you're right! But being right is not going to change people. If we were just intellects, it might be different. But these things are never just about intellectual and theological correctness. This doesn't mean you don't do your homework. It just means the chief value of your homework is more about your own sense of integrity than it is about changing the minds of others.

Second, keep in mind that the people at church who don't want to change are not your enemies. They are, most likely, your brothers and sisters in Christ. But even if they were your enemies, guess what? Jesus requires us to "love [our] enemies and pray for those who persecute [us]" (Matt. 5:44). Here's a good way to do a gut check on this. It's a little list entitled "How to Tell If You're Treating People like Enemies."

1. If you're gossiping about people, you are treating them like enemies.
2. If you're calling people names behind their back, you are treating them like enemies.
3. If you've stopped spending time with people other than to debate issues, you are treating them like enemies.
4. If you can no longer have a pleasant conversation with people, you are treating them like enemies.

What's more, just because the people with whom you disagree start treating you like an enemy does not give you permission to return the favor. A long time ago, at another church, I took an unpopular stand on an issue. A meeting was called to discuss it. When it was my turn to stand up and present my point of view, the people who disagreed with me booed. I had clearly become their enemy. Unfortunately, I allowed myself to be convinced that they were my enemies too. Not only was that unhelpful, but it also made things a whole lot worse. You might leap to my defense here and say that my response was only natural. You would be right. But we have supernatural resources available to us in times like that. Jesus will always help us do what he requires of us. Jesus will always model what he wants us to do. My problem was that I just didn't accept the offer.

BE THE CATALYST FOR CHANGE

We've talked a bit about what we can't do, so let's talk for a moment about what we can do. I came across a phrase a number of years ago. I don't remember who said it, but the person who did should get a Pulitzer Prize. The phrase is "critique by creating." Here's the idea: instead of referring to something you've experienced outside the church, as good as that is, think about creating some kind of experience inside the church. For example, let's say you served at a place like Atlanta Mission and just loved it. But it was something you did as an individual or with a small group of friends. It wasn't an activity your church had any investment in. Think about asking whichever staff member is in charge if you can organize a Saturday morning service day where the congregation is invited to go serve at the local homeless shelter. You're not asking the church to change; you're just asking for an opportunity. It's just an experiment, and if it doesn't go well, it will never happen again.

The odds that you'll be given permission to try something new increase if you offer to do all the legwork. If you served at the homeless shelter with friends, now is the time to "deputize" those friends to help you put on the event for the church. You'll coordinate with the shelter. You'll do the announcement. You'll arrange the sign-up process. You'll organize the transportation. Just make sure you do a competent job. If details aren't your thing, find someone who loves to handle details. You don't want this opportunity to be torpedoed by doing a sloppy job of administering things.

Here's a pro tip: if the church leaders balk at a new outreach project for the whole congregation, then ask if you can do it for the youth group. More than once, I've seen whole churches changed because something happened with their youth group that slowly began to affect the rest of the congregation. It usually started with the parents raving about how an experience changed their kids.

One last thing about being a change agent: We are only the agents of change. It is God who does the changing. We are just the people through whom he moves. Apparently, he's not picky about whom he chooses. One time he used a prostitute named Rahab. Another time he used a murderer and adulterer named David. One time he actually used a donkey (see Num. 22:27–31). I'm not commenting on your character or intelligence here. I'm just saying that it's ultimately about God, not us. He will use whomever he wants, and sometimes his choices are mysterious. Sometimes they don't make sense. Sometimes they even seem unwise to us. If we get picky here, it's good to remember that, at the end of the day, none of us are really qualified to be used by God. He makes choices based solely on his gracious decision to do so.

If you think about this, it will produce two things. The first is humility. We become humble because we realize we're not indispensable to the kingdom. It's not our agenda, our timetable, or our vision. It's God's. Change agents who have been activated by the kingdom have this paradoxical mixture of intentionality and surrender. It's our thing, but it's not. We are working hard but not carrying the weight of the responsibility. It's God's deal, not ours. We are change agents who are not responsible for change.

The second thing that happens when we realize our proper place in the process of change is this: we pray. We do so because it's only by depending on him that we will be able to navigate the turbulent waters of change without screwing things up. Apart from depending on him, we will probably make more of a mess than the mess we were trying to clean up in the first place.

The next time your church takes a right turn when you wish it had turned left or comes to a stop when you wanted it to start, don't leave too soon. Sure, there may come a time when God sends you somewhere else. But if and when that happens, you'll find yourself dealing with similar issues. Your new church will make some mistake that will drive you crazy. For some reason, God has chosen to entrust the church to people—broken, messy people. They'll be waiting for you at the next church and the one after that and the one after that. The good news is that wherever you go, you'll fit right in.

DISCUSSION QUESTIONS

1. Is your church interested in the experiences you've had out in the world moving toward the mess? On what do you base your answer?

2. Which side of the gospel does your church tend to emphasize—the personal side or the social side?

3. How can we start to minimize the influence of consumerism in the church?

4. What might be some legitimate reasons for leaving a church?

5. Of the various errors the author mentions regarding the facilitation of change, which one are you most prone to make?

6. What is meant by the statement "We are change agents who are not responsible for change"?

Chapter 16

DO I HAVE TO QUIT MY DAY JOB?

*Whether you make yourself available to a friend or
co-worker, or you make time every month to do volunteer
work, there is nothing that harvests more of a feeling of
empowerment than being of service to someone in need.*
—Gillian Anderson

It's time to address an important question. We've touched on it
already, but we need to dive in and get as clear on it as possible. Here's
the deal. After reading the stories about Bob Creson, Jim Reese, and
others in this book, some of you may be asking, "If I really want to
be committed to moving toward the mess, do I have to quit my job?
If I really want to make a difference, do I need to become a pastor or
work for a nonprofit?" The answer is no, you don't. Chances are that
you are right where God wants you. That means you are surrounded
by opportunity.

One reason God probably wants you to stay where you are
is that there's a mess he wants you to engage in where you work.
He's selected you for the job because you're already a part of that

culture and already have relationships with the people there. So it's way easier for you to connect with the problem than it would be to get somebody from the outside involved. An outsider would need to develop relationships and build trust. You've already done that.

As a result, he might want you to reach out to a former colleague who just lost her job. It could be that someone has an addiction of some sort and needs a safe person in whom to confide. There might be a single mom at your office struggling with raising her kids who needs your help. It could be any number of things. So if you're a teacher, keep on teaching. If you're an accountant, keep on counting. If you're a singer, keep on singing. If you're a baseball player, keep on swinging.

ALL ARE INVITED TO JOIN THE MESS

If you're a stay-at-home parent, this principle applies to you too. There's no need to change your status. You just need to look around. As a housewife or a househusband, you are strategically placed. It's no accident you are where you are. God has plans for you. Loneliness is rampant in suburban neighborhoods. There are people who would be thrilled if you would simply invite them to meet for coffee. There are others around you who have all the right stuff but are searching for some sort of meaning in their lives. You can be an invaluable resource as they struggle to make sense of things. Then there are parents who are worried about their kids. They need someone to talk to, someone to tell them that their kids are dealing with normal kid stuff. If you're available for God to use, you'll find your days are filled with chances to love people in your neighborhood as they struggle with what life has thrown at them.

Are you a student? There are people in your class, on your team, in your dorm, or at your lunch table who are not doing well. Some of them are at the bottom of your school's pecking order. But some are the cool people who everybody thinks are on top of the world. That's not always the case. If you have the courage to connect with these folks, you'll be surprised at what you find. You say you're just a kid? God uses kids all the time. Age makes no difference to him. It's all about availability.

Then there are the people over sixty-five. You are the fastest-growing demographic in the United States. Nobody gets to be your age without taking some hard knocks. When placed in God's hands, those tough times shape character and produce wisdom. In light of that, here's an interesting fact. Baby boomers (people born between 1946 and 1964) were famous back in the day for saying, "Don't trust anyone over thirty." But millennials (those born between 1982 and 1997) are different. They are interested in learning what older people have learned. If you're willing to listen and ask some good questions, you could have a significant impact. Millennials are living in a very messy world. You can help.

All of this is to say that the old aphorism "Bloom where you are planted" still holds true. Opportunity surrounds everybody. It's everywhere. We need never be bored another day in our lives. We need never worry about being too young or too old. We need never feel that we're missing something because we're stay-at-home parents. God is not concerned about age or vocation. He's just looking for someone to follow him out into the mess.

Then there are the myriad volunteer opportunities that pop up everywhere we look. Giving a few hours a month is an excellent example of faithfulness, regardless of what you do with the rest of your time. If enough of us thoughtfully invest our time in what God is doing in the world, we have a chance to create significant change. We have a chance to alter what our culture thinks about Christians and the church. We have a chance to see suffering and pain decline as God moves through us in the world.

A DIFFERENCE MAKER AMONG A MESS

Recently I met a man who gets all of this and is doing something about it. Meet Steve Kamerschen. Steve is the vice president of sales for his family's company. A graduate of the University of Georgia, he is happily married and has two daughters. He lives in a nice house and goes to church each Sunday. In other words, he's a pretty normal guy. But in his spare time, he's doing something extraordinary.

About a year ago, Steve watched a video played during a worship service at Buckhead Church. It gave the audience a glimpse into the plight of young children who are growing up in dangerous and impoverished circumstances. Because of this, the church had formed a partnership with an urban grade school. The video provided a link to a website where people could sign up to be mentors at that school. Steve jumped at the chance.

When he visited the school for the first time, he was dismayed. The school sits in the middle of a run-down neighborhood, surrounded by liquor stores, apartment buildings, and a lot of boarded-up homes.

Steve was paired with an eight-year-old first-grade boy. His mom called him "the J Man." This little guy was struggling academically and socially. The principal wondered if he might be bipolar. He had six brothers and sisters. His dad had recently gotten out of prison but hadn't returned home. It was indeed a messy situation.

Steve has been at it for a while now. Recently, he sent an email describing his experience to Buckhead Church staff member Cara Barfield, who administers the mentoring program there. I asked if I could share it with you. What follows is Steve's unvarnished email, with the names omitted to protect people's identities.

> Cara, I had been mentoring _____ for eight months and did not think I was making a difference. We got along well, but I did not feel like I was really getting to him. About three weeks ago, it really changed. He has asked me since day one to take him somewhere on a weekend. I told him I would, but I could never contact his mom as she had no phone. I know you and Dr. _____ [the school principal] and Ms. _____ [the boy's teacher] all tried to get a number or some kind of info for his mom or grandmother. Still no luck.
>
> Last time I went to mentor him at school, he asked me again (as he did each month) to take him to the zoo or somewhere on the weekend. I said yes, as I did each month but reminded him his mom had no phone. He said she now has one. I did not think much of it but an hour after I left his school,

my phone rang and it was his mom. She told me how much he liked it when I came to his school. She also said she would be glad for me to take him somewhere on Saturday.

Well, my eleven-year-old daughter has a division championship tennis match that same Saturday, but I knew this was the chance I had been waiting for. So I explained to my daughter I had to miss her match and go with _____ on Saturday. She understood.

When I went to pick him up (admittedly concerned based on the address), it was worse than I expected. About eight people appeared to be living at the apartment. There were mattresses on the floor, broken kitchen cabinet doors—just not nice at all. There were empty beer cans just outside the door, and men smoked dope one apartment above. His mom was there and was nice. We left, and he asked me if we could go eat, so we went up the street for breakfast.

We then went to the "Imagine It" children's museum. We had a great time. He asked to eat again, so we went to dinner. It breaks my heart that he needs food, something we take for granted. We had another outing, with his mom's permission, the following week. We went to the park and then out to eat. He kept telling me he wanted a white box this time. I finally figured out that last time I gave him a to-go container of food from the restaurant, and he wanted a white to-go box with food to take home again.

His mom texted me tonight and told me I was making a big difference in his life. Thanks so much for giving me the chance to connect with the "J Man," as his mom calls him. I am the winner in this whole thing.

I spoke with Steve the other day. He has met the J Man's brothers and sisters, most of whom are adolescents. He feels as if it's almost too late for them. They have been immersed in this dysfunctional culture for a long time. The prospects of change for them grow more remote by the day. However, he is hopeful about his little guy because he's so young. He thinks there is still a chance for a positive male role model to make a difference. It will be a steep uphill climb. But Steve is willing to make the journey. He has become one of my heroes.

So for all of you engineers, designers, salespeople, construction workers, professors, mechanics, fashion models, IT guys, students, housewives, and senior citizens ... God has you right where he wants you! Fasten your seat belt. If you'll let him, he will use you to make a powerful difference in the world, one person at a time. You are on the front lines. You have access to some people and situations that pastors and nonprofit employees just can't get to. You are making a difference. You are moving toward the mess. If you ever doubt that, just remember Steve and the J Man. The story you're writing can be every bit as poignant, messy, and fruitful. As a matter of fact, that's exactly what God has planned.

DISCUSSION QUESTIONS

1. Have you ever thought about quitting your job and going into church or nonprofit work? What did you decide? Why did you make that decision?

2. Why do people often think full-time ministry is a more godly vocation than most other jobs? Are they right? Why or why not?

3. What sorts of messes exist where you work? Is it easy or hard for you to get involved with them?

4. What's the difference between moving toward the mess and sticking your nose in other people's business?

5. Have you ever known or been involved with a family like the one Steve Kamerschen described? How did that come about? What happened?

6. If you were to take a next step toward the mess as a result of reading this chapter, what might it be?

Chapter 17

THE BIG B

Ultimately, burning out is just as unfaithful
as not doing anything at all.

—Anonymous

Sometimes things just come together. After some thought and prayer, you've developed some enthusiasm for serving. You've spent time researching all the possibilities and found just the right nonprofit. You're excited about the organization's focus, and it looks as though it will be a great fit for you. You've found four friends who want to serve with you. You all get along great and have a riotously good time whenever you're together. It looks as if everything's ready. On your mark … get set … go!

You start to see that you're making a difference. You're actually moving toward the mess. God is at work through you. The kingdom is accomplishing things because you and your friends show up each week. But it's more than that. He's at work in you as well. You are being transformed as you serve. From every angle, things are going very well.

As the weeks fly by, you start to notice something. There's a whole lot to do. Maybe you started by making sandwiches at the local rescue mission. Then you heard the staff needed someone to pick up the bread that the local supermarket donates on Tuesday evenings. Done. Then they needed someone to find a venue for the annual fund-raiser. You did it. Oh, and by the way, they want you to sponsor a table and find ten people to invite. Yikes! But you'll do it. You're in the zone. Then they need someone to drive the truck to pick up the new tables for the kitchen where the sandwiches are made. Um … you guess you could do that. And they want you to help work the phones next Friday night when they hold their tenth-annual phone-a-thon. What?

Six months go by. You wake up one day and realize you don't want to do this anymore. You start to drop out of things. By month seven, you are no longer involved. The passion is gone. Your calendar fills up with other things. You stop returning the nonprofit's phone calls. What happened? It's pretty simple. You tried to sprint through a marathon. That just doesn't work. Nobody can do that. And now you're burned out. Maybe you thought you were different. Maybe you thought God would prevent you from burning out because, after all, you were serving him. Sorry, but that's not the way it works.

So who's responsible for this? Not the nonprofit's staff. They will take as much as you'll give them. There's nobody who will say, "Hey, I noticed that Seth (or Audrey) is spending eight hours a week serving with us. I wonder if that's sustainable?" The nonprofit's staff have a mission to fulfill. They are, as they should be, focused on finding the resources to accomplish that mission. The question of sustainability is not their responsibility. That's your job.

THE NUMBERS DON'T ADD UP

Let's look at the math here. It will make it obvious that creating a sustainable pace is in everybody's best interests. Say you're serving at the local soup kitchen for eight hours a week, and after six months you burn out. Six months contain twenty-six weeks. So in your sprint you've contributed two hundred and eight hours before you collapsed in a heap. And it's likely that, after burning out, you won't be returning.

Let's say, on the other hand, that after some prayerful consideration, you decide you can sustain a pace of two hours a week indefinitely. Let's say you keep that up for four years before you decide to take a break. After some time off, you'll probably return because you've not reduced yourself to an oil spot on the rug. Four years contain two hundred and eight weeks. If you average two hours per week over a four-year period, you will have contributed around four hundred hours, given some time off for vacation and the occasional flu bug. That's about twice what you would have done at the burnout rate of serving, not to mention that, after a break, you'll probably be back for another multiyear stint. What's more, serving has become a part of the way you live your life. It has transitioned from being a short-term event to being a lifestyle. It has become one of the things that define who you are.

It's likely that this is not new information for you. I bet you've heard it before. We all understand the idea of burnout. It's not quantum mechanics. The vexing thing is that it's usually hard to recognize in your own life. Or maybe we do recognize it but are reluctant to admit it. In either case, by the time we figure it out or admit that it's happening, it's too late. The damage is done.

I have an idea about why this seems to be an especially common problem among Christians. But before we get to that, I want to give you a list—the seven signs of burnout.[1] I don't usually go for acronyms. They tend to be a bit cheesy. But despite the cheese factor, perhaps this will sound the alarm next time burnout starts to creep into your life. Watch for these signs:

> **B**ad attitude. This is self-explanatory.
>
> **U**nfulfilled. Serving ceases to be satisfying.
>
> **R**eactionary rather than proactive. You sit around waiting to be told what to do.
>
> **N**oncommunicative. You stop returning people's emails.
>
> **O**verly stressed. It's the feeling that you're carrying the world on your shoulders.
>
> **U**nmotivated. It's not that you don't have any energy—you just don't care.
>
> **T**ired. Fatigue becomes your new normal.

Everybody has the occasional bad day. So when a few of these pop up every once in a while, it's not time to panic. You'll probably be fine tomorrow. But if several of these signs start to become chronic, then it's time to do something. The place to start is admitting that you're burned out. The longer you wait, the worse it will get. At some point, if you refuse to do anything, your body will begin to protest. Your resistance to things like colds or flu will start to diminish. You might have trouble sleeping. But there's no need for those things to happen. The good news is that once you admit you have a problem, there are some practical steps you can take to remedy the situation and prevent it from happening again.

REGAIN BALANCE

First of all, it's time to take a break. But don't just disappear. Tell your group and the organization where you're volunteering what's going on. Assure them that you just need a little time to restore balance in your life. If the nonprofit tries to guilt you into continuing, stand firm and make your well-being a priority.

While you're on hiatus, it's important that you regain control of your calendar. It's pretty simple. Get out ahead of all the demands on your discretionary time. Look at the next several weeks coming up. Once you're far enough ahead, start to fill in your calendar openings, not with another round of commitments but with time off—scheduled free time when you can refill your tanks. Make sure to leave some blank spaces for volunteering. But don't fill those in yet.

Before you reschedule your volunteer time, it's important to prioritize. This will be difficult because you will feel as if everything's important. But if *everything* is important, then *nothing* is important. So make a list of all the ways you serve. In addition to the nonprofit, there may be some things you do at church. You might volunteer somewhere else through your job. Make sure the list is complete. Then go back through and rank everything. Give a "one" to your top priority, and so on.

The next step is called pruning. If you want to avoid burning out again, you're going to have to trim things off your list. The logical place to look will be at those things you've given a lower ranking or priority. Even so, you won't like doing this. It involves saying no to some good things. But remember, you're trying to create a sustainable pace. You're trying to stop sprinting through a marathon. Keep pruning until you've whittled down your list so that the items that remain can fit into the space you've allotted for volunteer work. Then once you've rested long enough, start the new schedule.

There's another essential step: once a quarter, schedule a half day or a full day away. Find a place to go where you can be alone to quietly reflect on the quality of your life over the previous three months. And here's the big challenge—resolve to turn off your phone for the day. You might argue that you need your phone to reflect on your life. No, you don't. Make hard copies of whatever calendars and journals you'll be reviewing. If you don't disconnect from your phone, not much will happen. After ten minutes, you'll find yourself checking your Instagram account or seeing who won the big game last night. So decide before you go—phone and other devices will be turned off and will stay off.

When I lived in Pasadena, California, I used to drive up to Mount Wilson, which defines the northern boundary of the Los Angeles Basin where thirteen million people live. There are several isolated places where you can sit and look out over metro LA. It's a stunning view. I would take some time up there to review my life and my calendar and make whatever adjustments seemed necessary. That process was extremely helpful. Then, as now, the practice of getting away once a quarter went a long way toward preventing burnout.

BEWARE OF RECURRING BURNOUT

If burnout has become a regular part of your life cycle—something that happens over and over again despite your best efforts—then you might want to consider getting with someone to figure out why this keeps happening. Enlist the help of a trusted friend, mentor, or counselor. In any case, make sure that you process this with someone. If you don't figure out how and why burnout keeps happening, the underlying causes will never be resolved. They won't go away on their own. They have to be identified and countered.

I mentioned that burnout seems to be unusually common among Christians. I think this has to do with a misunderstanding about the Christian life, and the confusion is often rooted in a well-known biblical text. In Luke 9:23, Jesus says, "If any man would come after me, let him deny himself and take up his cross daily and follow me." We mistakenly equate *denying ourselves* with *not taking good care of ourselves*. Additionally, we mistake the point of the metaphor Jesus uses here. We associate taking up our cross with wearing ourselves out. I don't believe that's what Jesus was trying to say. In fact, self-denial and taking up one's cross is made more difficult if we are not taking proper care of ourselves. Here's what I mean.

Self-denial is about defeating self-centeredness. It's about focusing on someone other than you. It's about taking yourself out of the center of your life and putting God there. Once he is in the center of your life, your job is to do his bidding. This calls for trust and courage. It's a scary step to hand over control of your life to God. There are little voices in your head that will push the panic button. They'll say, "What if he makes me miserable?" They'll say, "What if he asks me to do something I absolutely hate?" Those little voices can be quite persuasive. And those little voices are always wrong. It turns out God is really good at running our lives—much, much better than we are.

But here's the thing. If we're burned out or otherwise incapacitated, we're not going to be able to do what God asks, at least not very well. So it turns out that to deny yourself—that is, to put God in control of your life—you have to take care of yourself. This isn't some weird religious sort of thing. The same principle applies everywhere in life. If you're a fireman and don't stay in shape, you're not going to do a good job of rescuing people from burning houses. If you're a teacher and you're sick all the time, you're going to miss a lot of classroom time. That's just the way life works.

I know what you might be thinking: *What about that reference to the cross? How is that taking good care of myself?* I don't believe the point of the metaphor has to do with physical suffering; it has to do with the fact that consistently letting God be in control of our lives is hard and often painful. We will be religious. We will go to church. We will serve out in the community. We will do all of that stuff and more. Just don't ask us to surrender control of our lives! It's the one thing we humans don't want to do. It's like dying to ourselves. Actually, that's exactly what it is. And dying hurts. It kills. Which is why Jesus says in Luke 9:24, "For whoever would save his life [keeps control of his life] will lose it; and whoever loses his life for my sake [gives control of it to God], he will save it."

It needs to be said that, for certain people, putting God in control of their lives will lead to physical suffering. Sometimes it will even lead to death. But to make that the inevitable outcome of a life surrendered to Jesus Christ does not accurately reflect what Jesus meant in Luke 9. Physical suffering is possible, but it's not the norm. What is normal is the intense struggle we all undergo to surrender our lives to God daily. That is the deathlike experience he's talking about.

What does this all have to do with burnout? Many of us Christians think real faithfulness is always about suffering. So when we burn out, in a warped sort of way we are inwardly satisfied, thinking it's a sign of our faithfulness. "I am suffering for the Lord!" we boast. We drag along as all the joy and energy slowly leak out of our souls. Then things finally grind to a halt and we think, *Well, I guess this is just the way things are supposed to be.* Actually no. Burnout is not the way things are supposed to be.

Here's the point. You can't serve God fully and energetically if you're burned out. Jesus puts it this way: "Love your neighbor as yourself" (Mark 12:31). Faithfulness to this command means taking care of "yourself"—taking care of your physical, emotional, and spiritual needs. Burning out is a breakdown in this process. When we burn out, we're no longer moving toward the mess. We're merely creating another mess in the name of Jesus. And that … is just crazy.

DISCUSSION QUESTIONS

1. Have you ever found a serving opportunity that you were really excited about? What was it? Did you create a sustainable pace for your work?

2. As you reflect on the seven signs of burnout, how do you measure up? Are you in trouble or are you doing pretty well? Explain your answer.

3. Have you been through burnout before? What happened? How did you get back to normal?

4. If you've struggled with burnout, have you tried some of the author's ideas for addressing the problem? How did it go?

5. How is your struggle with giving control of your life to God going?

6. Now that you've thought through the issues surrounding burnout, do you agree with the quote at the beginning of the chapter? Why or why not?

Chapter 18

DO SOMETHING NOW

Then flew one of the seraphim to me, having in his hand a
burning coal which he had taken with tongs from the altar.
And he touched my mouth, and said: "Behold, this has touched
your lips; your guilt is taken away, and your sin forgiven." And
I heard the voice of the Lord saying, "Whom shall I send, and
who will go for us?" Then I said, "Here am I! Send me."
—Isaiah 6:6–8

How could this be any clearer? "Here am I! Send me." In a memorable paragraph, Isaiah lays out a pattern for us. Get forgiven and get going. Salvation, with all its eternal splendor and potential, also carries with it a purpose in this life. We are saved from our mess in order to move toward the mess of others. God sent his Son into the world, and now his Son sends us.

But if you've been bored for a while, allowing yourself to be sent might be problematic. Change can be difficult. We adapt and get used to things the way they are. We settle for the status quo. We discover that boredom is like glue—it tends to hold you in place. It doesn't matter what kind of church you attend. It doesn't matter how well the preacher does on Sunday morning. It doesn't matter if you label yourself an evangelical, a moderate, a charismatic, a progressive, or if you don't label yourself at all. The thing is, if you've been bored for a while, it's tempting to accept boredom as normal. In other words, if you've been bored for a while, you're probably stuck.

So if this is where you are, it's time to figure out how to come unglued. It's time to tuck all the stories and ideas you've encountered in this book under your arm and get going. That is, if you want to leave a boring Christian life behind. Let's assume that you do. Let's assume that you are saying, "Yes! Yes, I am ready to get unstuck. I am ready to come unglued!" What's the next step? Great question. Let me tell you another story.

LESSONS FROM THE ROCK WALL

Meet John Cowan. He is a lanky, affable outdoorsman. His family and mine have been friends for years and years. Back when we all lived in Southern California, my cousin Eric came for a visit. John suggested we go rock climbing. Not wanting to appear cowardly, I agreed. *How bad can it be?* I thought. John knew that neither my cousin nor I was a rock climber. He'd probably find a little ten-foot-high beginner cliff that we could scamper up and down for a while. Then we could go watch college football, which is what most American males think God intended for Saturday afternoons.

John Cowan, however, had something else in mind.

He told us to meet him at a certain place in the mountains above Ojai, which is about forty-five minutes inland from Ventura, our hometown. When we arrived at the rendezvous point, I got a little concerned. It was in the middle of a valley bordered on both sides by nearly vertical rock walls, a hundred and fifty to two hundred feet high. I couldn't seem to find the little ten-foot beginner cliff.

For that matter, I couldn't seem to find John either. This was because I was looking only at places where it was reasonable for John to be. All of a sudden, I heard John's voice. "Hey, Hambrick! I'm up here!"

"Up here" turned out to be a tree root jutting out of the side of the canyon wall a hundred feet above the road. That's where John sat. There was a series of brightly colored climbing ropes hanging from the tree root all the way down to the canyon floor. I figured the manufacturer made them in festive colors to take the edge off the sheer panic people like me would feel when we used them. John was grinning down at Eric and me. He looked like Jack Nicholson in *The Shining*. (If you're too young to know what Jack Nicholson looks like, then do an online search for "Jack Nicholson Shining." You'll see a really creepy picture of him as he's about to try to kill someone.)

All of a sudden, John seemingly leaped off the tree root and, using the ropes, basically hopped down the side of the cliff until he was standing right next to us. He called it repelling. I agreed. He reached into his backpack and pulled out a jumble of thick nylon straps—climbing harnesses. You put these on and they connect you to the climbing ropes so you won't fall. You put them on below your belt, over your pants. I don't mind telling you they were a snug fit. Apparently, rock climbing includes personal humiliation in addition to mind-numbing fear.

After a few words of instruction, John scampered back up the rock face and resumed his position straddling the tree root. He would manage the ropes, so that if Eric or I fell, we wouldn't fall very far.

Eric went first. It turns out he was pretty good at finding the footholds and handholds needed to climb up the rock face. After about twenty minutes, he arrived at the tree root. With a high five, he repelled back down and landed back where he started. Then it was my turn.

It turns out the genes that made rock climbing so easy for Eric had not made it to my side of the family. The handholds and footholds that Eric had used turned out to be little rifts in the rock wall sometimes no more than an inch wide. I had no success with them. I kept slipping. After fifteen minutes, I was still on the canyon floor. I'll never forget what John said next.

"Look, if you want to be able to stick to those footholds and handholds, you're going to have to increase the traction on your fingertips and toes."

"Okay," I replied. "How do I do that?"

"You have to lean away from the wall," he explained.

"What?" I asked.

"You heard me," he said helpfully.

That struck me as utterly crazy talk. When you're scared of falling, you want to hug the wall, not lean away from it. It seemed like a surefire way to fall even more than I was already falling. But I didn't have anything to lose, so I tried it.

I was shocked. It was as if someone had coated my fingertips and boot toes with glue. I stuck where moments before I had fallen. It was magic. Within about twenty minutes, I was sitting on the tree root a hundred feet up the side of the canyon wall. I felt like a million bucks. Now John Cowan wasn't the only one smiling up there on that tree root.

GET SET TO CLIMB HIGHER

There are just a few points bundled into this story that I want to make sure you don't miss. First of all, think of leaning away from the wall as a metaphor. It's counterintuitive. It seems wrong, but it's exactly right. It's the one thing you don't want to do, but it turns out to be the only way you can get where you want to go.

Recall the words of Jesus: "For whoever would save his life will lose it; and whoever loses his life for my sake, he will save it" (Luke 9:24). This is also counterintuitive. The thing you think will work (saving your life) won't. And the thing you think won't work (losing your life for his sake) will. Things like serving the homeless may seem like another tedious "church thing" to you. It might sound to you like something that will make your life worse. It appears to represent something that will steal time and energy away from the things that will make your life more exciting. It's just like leaning away from the wall. It seemed like a bad idea, but it turned out to be a great idea. In fact, it was the only idea that worked. At first, I thought both John Cowan and Jesus were wrong. But much to my surprise, both of them were right.

The next thing I want you to consider is this: If you want to come unglued, maybe you need to find your version of John Cowan (or maybe in your case, a "Jenny" Cowan). Maybe you need that person who will challenge you, encourage you, and show you how to move toward the mess. God never intended for you to figure this out all by yourself. So look around. Your version of John Cowan is probably already in your life. He's that guy who's smiling all the time. He's that guy who is excited about his faith and is making a difference in the world. And the crazy thing is, he's having a great time doing it. He's having an adventure following Jesus. So go find this guy and let him show you the ropes (sorry, I couldn't resist the pun). I predict your boredom will soon be a thing of the past.

While you're at it, find your version of Eric (or "Erica") too. Find that younger person who is looking for someone a little farther down the road, someone to help him figure out what following Jesus looks like. Make a commitment to banish the spiritual boredom in his or her life. That will go a long way toward banishing the spiritual boredom in your life. Volunteer with your church youth group. Get involved with Young Life. Connect your version of Eric with your version of John Cowan. Watch out, though. You get the Erics of the world connected with the John Cowans of the world, and things will start to happen. You might end up with a movement on your hands. That could be a game changer for everybody.

As you consider all your options, don't set your sights too low. If I'd climbed only the little ten-foot training cliff I was looking for at first, I wouldn't have a story worth telling. It would have been too easy. It wouldn't have been challenging. It would have been boring. The principle here is this: you can't dispel boredom from your life with another boring experience. So whatever you're considering, make sure it's more like a scary hundred-foot cliff than a little rock you can scamper up without even raising your heart rate.

Finally, if this all makes sense to you, let's get going. Let's do something right now. I mean *right now*. The time has come to make a change. The longer you let that glue hold you in place, the harder it will be to break free. So pick up the phone. Call John Cowan. If you can't get a hold of him, go online and sign up to volunteer at that local homeless shelter. Or get up and walk across the street and check in with your hurting neighbor. Or hop in your car and drive over to that assisted-living center and strike up a conversation with one of the World War II veterans over there.

Life looks a whole lot better when you're sitting on a tree root a hundred feet up the canyon wall than it does standing on the canyon floor wishing you were up there. You'll see things up there that you've never seen before. You'll feel fully alive. You'll feel free. And all you have to do to get there is to lean away from the wall and start climbing. There's always room for one more up on the tree root. Maybe that could be you.

DISCUSSION QUESTIONS

1. If boredom has become glue for someone, do you think other factors such as laziness or fear might be involved? Why or why not?

2. Do you know someone like John Cowan? How did you meet him? What role does he play in your life?

3. If there isn't a John Cowan in your life right now, how would you go about finding one? How would you go about finding an Eric?

4. Of all the things you could try doing when it comes to moving toward the mess, which ones fall into the category of the little ten-foot rock? Which ones are more like the hundred-foot cliff?

5. If you are already moving toward the mess, congratulations! Is there a next step to take as you continue to follow Jesus in that direction? What might that be?

6. If you're reading this book with a group of people, is there something your group could do together in terms of moving toward the mess?

NOTES

INTRODUCTION

1. "Six Reasons Young Christians Leave Church," Barna Group, September 27, 2011, www.barna.org/barna-update/millennials/528-six-reasons-young-christians -leave-church#.

CHAPTER 2: THE HEART OF THE MATTER

1. Thanks to Bruce Deel, founder of City of Refuge (cityofrefugeatl.org) in Atlanta, Georgia, for this phrase.

CHAPTER 4: HOT DOGS AND PRAYERS

1. Leroy and Janelle have asked us to change the names of the two women whose stories we will tell in this chapter.
2. "About," That Grace Restored, www.thatgracerestored.com/about.

CHAPTER 8: STAYING IN PAKISTAN

1. "Rehan and Amreen," interview with the author, February 9, 2015.
2. "Global Terrorism Index 2014: Measuring and Understanding the Impact of Terrorism," Institute for Economics and Peace, www.visionofhumanity.org/sites /default/files/Global%20Terrorism%20Index%20Report%202014_0.pdf.

3. "Rehan and Amreen."

4. Patrick Johnstone, *Operation World: When We Pray God Works* (Waynesboro, GA: Paternoster, 2001), 500.

5. Winfried Corduan, *Pocket Guide to World Religions* (Downers Grove, IL: InterVarsity Press, 2006), 82.

6. "Global Terrorism Index 2014."

CHAPTER 9: CHANGE YOUR MIND, CHANGE YOUR WORLD

1. Andy Stanley, *Deep and Wide: Creating Churches Unchurched People Love to Attend* (Grand Rapids, MI: Zondervan, 2012), 58.

CHAPTER 10: NO MORE BORED KIDS

1. "Facts at Your Fingertips," Young Life, www.younglife.org/ResourceLibrary/Pages/Resources/FactsAtYourFingertips.aspx.

2. "Reaching a World of Kids," Young Life, www.younglife.org/RWOK/Pages/About.aspx.

3. "Out There in the World of Kids," Joshua Young Life, https://joshua.younglife.org/Pages/AboutYL.aspx.

4. "About Young Life," Young Life, www.younglife.org/About/Pages/default.aspx.

CHAPTER 11: BOB CRESON AND WYCLIFFE BIBLE TRANSLATORS

1. "Bible Statistics," United Fellowship Outreach Ministries, Inc., www.unitedfellowshipoutreach.com/Biblestatistics.html.

2. "Word Counts: How Many Times Does a Word Appear in the Bible?" Christian Bible Reference Site, www.christianbiblereference.org/faq_WordCount.htm.

3. Kenneth Scott Latourette, *A History of Christianity, Vol. 1: Beginnings to 1500* (Revised) (New York: HarperOne, 1975), 666.

4. Latourette, *A History of Christianity*, 666.

5. Ruth A. Tucker, *Parade of Faith: A Biographical History of the Christian Church* (Grand Rapids, MI: Zondervan, 2011), 205.

6. For a fuller description of these events, see Bob Creson, *The Finish Line: Stories of Hope through Bible Translation*, with Carol Schatz (Orlando, FL: Wycliffe USA, 2014), 64f.

7. Based on conversations with Bob and Dallas Creson in their home, January 30, 2015.

8. Creson, *The Finish Line*, 2–3.

9. Conversations with Bob and Dallas Creson.

10. Intercristo merged with ChristianJobs.com in 2009. See https://intercristo .wordpress.com/2009/03/18/intercristo-merges-with-christianjobs/.

11. Creson, *The Finish Line*, 143.

12. Creson, *The Finish Line*, 96.

CHAPTER 12: WHERE TO START?

1. "Quick Facts about Nonprofits," National Center for Charitable Statistics, November 2015, http://nccs.urban.org/statistics/quickfacts.cfm.

2. Charles Dickens, *The Readings of Charles Dickens* (London: Chapman & Hall, 1883), 4.

CHAPTER 13: WORK TOGETHER

1. Howard S. Friedman and Leslie R. Martin, *The Longevity Project: Surprising Discoveries for Health and Long Life from the Landmark Eight-Decade Study* (New York: Hudson Street Press, 2011), 17.

CHAPTER 14: JIM REESE AND ATLANTA MISSION

1. Atlanta Mission, http://atlantamission.org.

2. "2013 Annual Report," Atlanta Mission: Our City Our Mission, http://issuu.com /anniegomes/docs/fy13_annual_report, 19.

3. "2013 Annual Report," 19.

CHAPTER 17: THE BIG B

1. These are loosely based on the article by Lisa M. Gerry "10 Signs You're Burning Out—and What to Do about It," *Forbes*, April 1, 2013, www.forbes.com/sites/learnvest/2013/04/01/10-signs-youre-burning-out-and-what-to-do-about-it/.